SCIENTIFIC AMERICAN EXPLORES BIG IDEAS

Our Nuclear Future

Published in 2026 by Scientific American Educational Publishing
in association with **The Rosen Publishing Group**
2544 Clinton Street, Buffalo NY 14224

Contains material from Scientific American®, a division of Springer Nature America, Inc., reprinted by permission, as well as original material from The Rosen Publishing Group®.

First Edition

Scientific American
Lisa Pallatroni: Project Editor

Rosen Publishing
Michael Hessel-Mial: Compiling Editor
Michael Moy: Senior Graphic Designer

Cataloging-in-Publication Data

Names: Scientific American, Inc.
Title: Our nuclear future / edited by the Scientific American Editors.
Description: Buffalo, New York : Scientific American Educational Publishing, an imprint of Rosen Publishing, 2026. | Series: Scientific American explores big ideas | Includes glossary and index.
Identifiers: ISBN 9781538313046 (pbk.) | ISBN 9781538313053 (library bound) | ISBN 9781538313060 (ebook) Subjects: LCSH: Nuclear energy--Juvenile literature. | Nuclear power plants–Juvenile literature.
Classification: LCC TK9148.O97 2026 | DDC 333.792'4–dc23

Manufactured in the United States of America
Websites listed were live at the time of publication.

Cover: koto_feja/iStockphoto.com
Credit: Sébastien Philippe, Svitlana Lavrenchuk and Ivan Stepanov (132,133,134)

CPSIA Compliance Information: Batch # CSSA26.
For Further Information contact Rosen Publishing at 1-800-237-9932.

CONTENTS

INTRODUCTION

Of the fundamental modern science discoveries, few are quite so grand and terrible as the unlocking of the energy in the atom. The same intense energy that powers our sun can now be put to work on Earth, as domestic energy sources or as weapons. The Cold War (sometimes called the "atomic age"), which lasted from 1945 to 1991, was characterized by this grandeur and terror. Nuclear energy powered many of the wealthy countries in the world, with a small number of major, widely publicized plant meltdowns. Meanwhile, rival powers created vast stockpiles of nuclear weapons, which threatened the entire planet.

Today, people are debating whether to build more nuclear power plants as a response to climate change. In parallel, others are debating whether to expand the U.S. nuclear arsenal, with the aim of countering the country's rival, China. While much of the science and technology is well established, the policy is not. Unlike most topics in these volumes, there is significant disagreement over the necessity and safety of nuclear technology, especially nuclear power. In this title, the editor has attempted to represent these conflicting views, especially from perspectives that haven't always been included in the debate.

This book is organized into the following section topics: nuclear history, new power plant designs, nuclear power as climate solution, safety risks, nuclear waste, nuclear weapons, and nuclear physics.

These selections are meant to appeal to a wide range of interests in nuclear research. Physicists and engineers who wish to build power plants or design nuclear rockets to Mars will find much of interest. Environmentalists interested in the strengths and drawbacks of nuclear power can sharpen their judgments on this difficult topic. People interested in social justice can read the perspectives of communities impacted by nuclear mining and testing, especially those on U.S. Indian reservations, Africa, and the Pacific Islands.

As you read, you'll find that while our nuclear future isn't always clear, it is always fascinating, and it is still in our hands to shape.

Section 1: Our Nuclear Past

What Was the Manhattan Project?

By Tom Metcalfe; edited by Jeanna Bryner

The Manhattan Project was a top-secret program to make the first atomic bombs during World War II. Its results had profound impacts on history: the subsequent nuclear arms race has radically changed the political world order in ways that are still evident today.

Thousands of scientists, including theoretical physicist J. Robert Oppenheimer, took part in the Manhattan Project, often while they and their families were lodged at secret military bases in remote locations. It resulted in the two atomic bombs dropped on the Japanese cities of Hiroshima and Nagasaki in August 1945, which brought World War II to its end and probably killed more than 100,000 people.

"The Manhattan Project harnessed the enormous energy in the nucleus of the atom for the first time," explains Cynthia Kelly, founder and president of the Atomic Heritage Foundation, a nonprofit dedicated to the history of the project and the atomic age.

One of the project's consequences was the creation of terrifying opposing arsenals of nuclear weapons. But it also resulted in innovations from medicine to space exploration and in the science and engineering of civilian nuclear energy, Kelly says.

The U.S. Army Corps of Engineers created the Manhattan Engineer District in June 1942 to hide the development of the atomic bomb during the war–hence that effort's name of the "Manhattan Project."

But historian of science Alex Wellerstein explains in an online overview that the project originated in an idea from the late 1930s–that Nazi Germany might build an atomic bomb, so the U.S. should do so first. Historical records reveal that Germany didn't get far, but the prospect of a Nazi bomb was horrifyingly real.

Several leading researchers worked for wartime Germany, including Werner Heisenberg. Even so, many scientists who favored an American atom bomb, including Hungarian-born physicist Leo Szilard, had fled the Nazis in Europe.

In July 1939 Szilard and others enlisted the help of the renowned physicist Albert Einstein, then on holiday on Long Island, N.Y., to support them by writing a letter to President Franklin D. Roosevelt. The Einstein-Szilard letter, as it's known, changed history. It prompted Roosevelt to convene a committee to investigate the possibility of building an atomic bomb, and in 1941 this group became a new committee to lay the groundwork for the full project. These early stages involved key contributions from the U.K. and Canada. But in the end, the atomic bomb was mostly an American weapon.

After 1942 the Manhattan Project was the recognized Allied effort to build an atomic bomb. It mainly used uranium ore from a mine in what is now the Democratic Republic of the Congo, which was kept secret from the Germans.

Otherwise the project was conducted in the U.S., primarily at three top-secret towns: Oak Ridge, Tenn., where uranium was enriched until it was radioactive enough for nuclear fission; Hanford, Wash., where reactors transformed uranium into plutonium, an even more powerful nuclear fuel; and Los Alamos, N.M., where Oppenheimer directed the laboratory that designed and built experimental atomic bombs.

There were also dozens of smaller sites. And officials went to extraordinary lengths to keep it all secret.

World War II historian Alexandra Levy says most of the more than 600,000 people involved–including the thousands of scientists, engineers and technicians who worked on the weapons, as well as construction workers and the people who kept the three secret towns going–were deliberately not told their purpose.

"Most of those people did not know that the goal of the project was to build a new type of bomb," Levy says. "Today, between the Internet and social media, it's difficult to imagine such a large-scale endeavor remaining secret for long."

Kelly adds, "We live in a very, very different world. Aside from one or two key senators agreeing to a blank check for the Manhattan Project, Congress and the press were kept in the dark. That would be impossible today."

The Manhattan Project culminated in the Trinity test in New Mexico on July 16, 1945–the first detonation of a nuclear weapon. By that time, the U.S. had spent around $2.2 billion–the equivalent of around $37 billion today.

But the dangers of a Nazi bomb had faded, and Japan was now the designated target. Although Japan never had an atomic bomb program, the idea of stopping its aggression with a show of awful destruction became fixed among Manhattan Project leaders, science historian Wellerstein says.

He notes that Oppenheimer, then the charismatic director of the Los Alamos laboratory, twice voted in favor of the initial atomic bomb attack on Hiroshima –which killed tens of thousands of civilians–instead of a purely military target.

Oppenheimer is seen as essential to the success of the American atomic bomb project. "He contributed to some of the early scientific breakthroughs of the project," Levy says. "His great gift was bringing together scientists, engineers and other technicians to collaborate on and solve problems."

But Oppenheimer was also ambivalent about its results. In recalling his experience at the Trinity test in 1965, he quoted a story from the Hindu scripture the Bhagavad Gitaabout a prince, reluctant to kill his enemies, who witnessed the transformation of Krishna, an incarnation of the Hindu deity Vishnu: "Now I am become Death, the destroyer of worlds."

Oppenheimer was the reluctant prince, not Krishna. "He didn't want to kill people," Wellerstein says. "But he knew that nuclear weapons were going to be built anyway, and he felt that he had a duty to do this horrible thing."

About the Author

Tom Metcalfe is a freelance journalist who is based in London. Metcalfe writes mainly about science, space, archaeology, Earth and the oceans. He has also written for Live Science, the BBC, NBC News, National Geographic, Air & Space and many others.

Manhattan Project Plutonium, Lost to Obscurity, Recovered by Scientists

By Andy Extance

"Fat Man," the atomic bomb dropped by the U.S. on Nagasaki, Japan, in 1945, carried about 6.2 kilograms of enriched plutonium, roughly the size of a softball. The origin of that deadly hunk of metal can be traced back via a tiny sliver weighing less than three millionths of a gram, created in the labs of Manhattan Project researchers. It is a historic fragment, embodying both stunning scientific achievement and deep tragedy—that one bomb killed and wounded at least 64,000 people (estimates vary) as well as hastened Japan's surrender. And in 2007 this historic sample, the first plutonium ever seen by researchers, vanished from the public eye.

Now it has resurfaced in a plastic box in a windowless, secure six-foot by six-foot room in the University of California, Berkeley's Hazardous Material Facility. The tiny lump, derived from Nobel Prize–winning chemist Glenn Seaborg's original discovery of the element, was accompanied by only limited documentation about its origins. But a Berkeley team has found radioactive fingerprints indicating the sliver indeed comes from the Manhattan Project. They published their findings on the arXiv physics preprint server on December 24, and are now pushing to return this bit of history to public display.

The sliver's story starts in 1941, when the world's warring powers were racing to develop an atomic bomb, focusing largely on nuclear fission of uranium. At Berkeley that year, Seaborg, along with Arthur Wahl and Joseph Kennedy, synthesized an entirely new element: plutonium. Although they only produced vanishingly small traces of it by bombarding uranium 238 with deuterons—particles made of one proton and one neutron—they quickly determined it had explosive potential as nuclear bomb material.

By the start of 1942, scientists studying the nuclear chain reaction, such as physicist Enrico Fermi, and plutonium chemistry, such as Seaborg, were ordered to the University of Chicago to begin the work of the A-bomb–developing Manhattan Project. (Seaborg wrote about synthesizing plutonium, and several other elements, for *Scientific American* in an April 1950 article that includes a grainy photograph of one sample made in Chicago.)

Because plutonium had only just been discovered, the scientists had little idea of its properties. They needed more of the element to learn how to use it in a nuclear weapon. To make a larger amount and move beyond the difficulties of studying radioactive metal mixtures containing infinitesimally tiny amounts of plutonium, a group led by Seaborg fired neutrons at hundreds of pounds of uranium salts.

After a series of purification steps, Chicago chemists Burris Cunningham and Lewis Werner could then extract small amounts of plutonium salt from the original material. These salts, however, trapped a little water within their crystal structure. By burning the salts in air–and therefore reacting them with oxygen–the scientists created a water-free plutonium oxide. For the first time they were able to put their pure compound onto a specially made scale and record that they had isolated 2.77 micrograms worth. "They could actually see it," says U.C. Berkeley nuclear engineer Eric Norman, who performed some of the new tests to identify the sample's origins. "No one had ever seen plutonium before."

"That size specimen was quite a hunk in those very early days," says Cynthia Kelly, founder of the Atomic Heritage Foundation in Washington, D.C. "It cost hundreds of millions of dollars to produce even small quantities." That sample and the methods that produced it would, over the next three years, help advance plutonium science far enough to make the Fat Man bomb. (The Hiroshima bomb, dropped a few days earlier, had a uranium core.)

Seaborg was awarded the Nobel in 1951 for synthesizing plutonium and other elements beyond uranium, extending the periodic table. The University of Chicago gave him the original 2.77-microgram plutonium sample to keep, encased in a transparent plastic box. ("The amount of radioactivity in this sample is incredibly low and is not a health hazard to anybody," Norman says.) Seaborg then gave it to the Lawrence Hall of Science at U.C. Berkeley, which displayed it in a glass case starting in 1979, alongside a simple placard describing its origins. Then in 2007 staff removed the box in favor of more interactive exhibits during a display makeover. The container languished in storage with little indication of its importance.

In 2008 Phil Broughton, a U.C. Berkeley health physicist, spotted a clear plastic box labelled "First sample of Pu weighed. 2.7 μg" while checking the Hazardous Material Facility's inventory. Broughton says he was shocked to attention because a placard citing Seaborg's work was sitting right next to the box. "This is the equivalent to the original moon rock," he enthuses. But with no other evidence accompanying the box, he feared its contents would be forgotten.

For several years it seemed Broughton's fears were justified. For example, he asked the Smithsonian Institution in Washington, D.C., if that museum wanted it. Curators there, however, wanted Broughton to give them proof this was definitely the 1942 sample, and he had none besides the loose placard, which was not exactly scientific evidence. The box stayed in its windowless prison.

In July 2014 Broughton asked Berkeley's Department of Nuclear Engineering for help in identifying the metal. Norman, along with fellow nuclear engineer Keenan Thomas and Kristina Telhami–a summer undergraduate research assistant from San Diego State University–stepped forward to test the sample. They carefully searched for the "fingerprints" of plutonium decaying to uranium–gamma rays emitted by atomic nuclei and x-rays emitted by electrons–using a germanium ionization detector.

The Berkeley team's measurements showed the sample is definitely high-purity plutonium. They also detected other clues pointing to its Manhattan Project origin. Seaborg's approach had only produced plutonium 239, which decays very slowly back to uranium 238. Later production of plutonium, done by bombarding uranium with neutrons in nuclear reactors, sometimes also produces plutonium 241, which decays more rapidly to the element americium. There is no sign of americium in the Berkeley sliver.

The scientists estimate the sample has a plutonium mass of 1.7 to 2.3 micrograms. That is "remarkably" close to what would be left after subtracting the mass of oxygen contained in the original plutonium oxide, Norman says. An x-ray signal corresponding to a reaction vessel made out of platinum, which was the type Cunningham and Werner used, also points to the salvaged sample.

At the moment the plastic box remains in the custody of Broughton and his colleagues. Norman hopes it will be displayed in the very same Berkeley chemistry laboratory where Seaborg's team made their original momentous discovery. The university's chemistry department is keen to have the sample. Seaborg's lab is still being used for research, however, so space constraints could keep it from becoming the site of a permanent exhibit.

Kelly agrees that displaying the plutonium in a lab-cum-museum would be a great idea, noting that Berkeley could also become part of a new Manhattan Project National Historical Park, which includes many of the project's original facilities. Pres. Barack Obama signed a law authorizing the park at the end of last year. Such recognition would seem an appropriate reflection of the artifact's impact: only rarely has something so slight had repercussions reverberating so far into the future.

About the Author

Andy Extance is a freelance science writer based in Exeter, England, who protests with Extinction Rebellion and Just Stop Oil. He is accredited as a chartered chemist and chartered scientist by the Royal Society of Chemistry.

Nuclear-Testing 'Downwinders' Speak about History and Fear

By Sarah Scoles; edited by Clara Moskowitz

When Sandra Evans Walsh was growing up in Parowan, Utah, her class would sometimes trek outside to a row of trees. They were about to watch history in the making, the teacher would tell them. The kids would then stare as an orange shroud spread across the sky. "I remember the clouds coming over our town and writing our names in the dust," she said in an interview with Justin Sorensen, a geographical information systems (GIS) specialist at the University of Utah's J. Willard Marriott Library.

That dust had traveled around 200 miles, all the way from what is now called the Nevada National Security Site, where scientists once tested nuclear weapons. Between 1945 and 1962, U.S. researchers detonated around 200 bombs aboveground–100 of them in Nevada. Fallout from the nuclear tests–radioactive particles that were swept into the atmosphere and fell back down to the earth–found their way into crops and livestock, whose radioactivity humans took on when they consumed milk, meat and produce. Fallout takes many different chemical forms, one of which is iodine-131: an isotope, or version, of iodine that has the usual 53 protons but 78 neutrons instead of the standard 74. Inside the body, the thyroid gland will absorb iodine-131, which eventually decays to produce radiation that can cause thyroid cancer and other problems.

People, such as Walsh, who lived "downwind" of nuclear development and open-air explosions are now called "downwinders." Mary Dickson, another downwinder, told Sorensen and one of his colleagues that she thought the attitude toward those in Utah who were affected by nuclear testing was, "you know, 'They were Mormons and cowboys and Indians–who cares?'" In general, she added, "they test where they think there are populations that don't matter."

Sorensen and his team spoke to both women and dozens of other people for a project called the Downwinders of Utah Archive. Hosted by the J. Willard Marriott Library, the archive is an attempt to qualify, quantify and make accessible people's experiences of, and effects from, the American legacy of nuclear weapons testing. In 2011 the Senate unanimously designated January 27 as the National Day of Remembrance for Downwinders. "The downwinders paid a high price for the development of a nuclear weapons program for the benefit of the United States," stated the resolution establishing the designation.

But when the tests were conducted, no one had done the research necessary to truly calculate what that price would be. Wanting to understand the potential link between regional health issues and fallout from nuclear tests, the National Cancer Institute (NCI) undertook a study on Americans exposed to iodine-131 from the Nevada tests. The results were released in 1997 in a report entitled "Estimated Exposures and Thyroid Doses Received by the American People from Iodine-131 in Fallout following Nevada Atmospheric Nuclear Bomb Tests." It was this document that first led Sorensen to the archival project. "We were just kind of wondering, originally, 'What does this data look like if you put it on a map?'" he says, "because a spreadsheet doesn't really tell you a lot." Sorensen's background is in GIS and cartography, so he took the NCI's fallout data and overlaid them onto his home state. "It just really grew from there," he says. "We started seeing there's a story to be told."

That story, Sorensen knew, included individual human narratives. So he and his team used their maps to pinpoint hotspots in the Beehive State. Advertising in heavily dosed places, such as St. George and Cedar City, the archivists asked people to come to their local libraries and share their experiences. "We came back with 30-plus interviews," Sorensen says.

Some interviewees told Sorensen of men who examined their thyroids or of the potassium iodide pills teachers passed out to combat the effects of radiation. Dickson recalled watching public-information films starring *Bert the Turtle*, who taught kids to duck and cover in the event of a nuclear explosion. The film, though, was not really a warning about what your own country might do inside its borders.

Alongside the interviews, Sorensen collected hard geospatial data and analysis. Web visitors to his archive can survey iodine fallout maps, diagrams of mushroom-cloud heights for different test series, animations of nuclear air drops, milk consumption statistics from when contaminated cows passed their burden on and an interactive timeline of the explosive atomic age. "I was really surprised just how closely and accurately the interviews match the data," Sorensen says. In particular, he cites a test in the Operation Upshot-Knothole series. Later the test was nicknamed "Dirty Harry" because it generated more fallout than any other continental boom, much of which ended up near St. George. "You hear this firsthand, and it brings all the information together," he says.

Although no single illness can be conclusively tied to a test-site cause, investigations by the United Nations Scientific Committee on the Effects of Atomic Radiation and the International Physicians for the Prevention of Nuclear War and the Institute for Energy and Environmental Research, among others, have established links between radiation exposure and cancer occurrence. In the early 2000s a report by NCI and the Centers for Disease Control and Prevention estimated that fallout could have led to around 11,000 excess deaths. The NCI has also created a calculator that allows users to calculate their thyroid dose and risk of developing thyroid cancer from fallout. "We can't know any individual's cancer was caused by radioactivity," explains Scott Williams, former executive director of HEAL Utah, a nonprofit advocacy group focused on the environment and public health, "but we do know that some people's cancer risk was increased by radioactivity."

Since 1990 the federal government has offered some recompense to downwinders and others affected by nuclear testing through the Radiation Exposure Compensation Act (RECA). Set to expire this summer unless a bill is passed to renew (and expand) it, RECA pays downwinders, test participants and uranium workers between \$50,000 and \$100,000–if they have specific ailments and can prove (with decades-old evidence that is sometimes hard to come by) they were in the wrong place at the wrong time. "We left a burden on unwitting citizens across the country without ever informing them," Williams says. "We need to do the honorable thing and own the problem and not create these problems again."

The Downwinders of Utah Archive is always expanding, and though Sorensen paused interviews during the pandemic, he plans to light the fuse again soon. He also hopes to expand the project to other Western states to preserve their history, too.

Making sure that information remains accessible is part of the point of the Downwinders of Utah Archive. The day of remembrance is, in its own way, an isotope of that openness. "Those kind of markers are really important...," Dickson told Sorensen and his colleague. "Otherwise, you know, time marches on, and it's like dipping a big spoon in the water. The rest of the water just fills in, and it's like it was never there."

This reporting was supported by the International Women's Media Foundation's Howard G Buffett Fund for Women Journalists.

About the Author

Sarah Scoles is a Colorado-based science journalist, a contributing editor at Scientific American and a senior contributor at Undark. Her newest book is Countdown: The Blinding Future of Nuclear Weapons (Bold Type Books, 2024).

The U.S. Must Take Responsibility for Nuclear Fallout in the Marshall Islands

By Hart Rapaport & Ivana Nikolić Hughes

Russia's placement of its nuclear arsenal on high alert during the war in Ukraine has unearthed fears of nuclear holocaust. As governments across the world consider their own roles in lessening the risk of nuclear war, the U.S. cannot excuse itself. We should talk about stemming a future nuclear impact, but equally important is reckoning with our past.

Between 1946 and 1958 the U.S. nuclear testing program drenched the Marshall Islands with firepower equaling the energy yield of 7,000 Hiroshima bombs. Cancer rates have doubled in some places, displaced people have waited decades to return to their homes, and radiation still plagues the land and waters of this Pacific island nation. The U.S. must prioritize the restoration of these islands and the resettlement of their people as a matter of human rights and environmental justice. What the U.S. has done so far is simply not enough.

The tests most gravely affected four atolls in the north of the nation: Bikini, Enewetak, Rongelap and Utirik. In the first two cases, members of the U.S. military resettled communities prior to testing, whereas people on Rongelap and Utirik left after fallout from tests reached them. Today only Enewetak and Utirik have substantial permanent populations; refugees from Bikini and Rongelap are still unable to return home safely.

In addition, the structural integrity of the Runit Dome, a concrete shell covering more than 100,000 cubic yards of nuclear waste on an island of Enewetak Atoll, is at risk because of rising sea levels. Leakage from the dome will likely increase, and higher tides threaten to break the structure open.

To better understand the effect of nuclear testing on the islands, scientists at the Department of Energy have conducted a wide range of studies. We believe their work has missed critical pieces. Rather than taking simple, direct measurements of gamma radiation, the DOE has consistently relied on simulations. Still, the military has notably cleaned up some parts of Enewetak Atoll.

For several years our group has gone to the Marshall Islands to research the fallout of this nuclear testing. We have published our findings to ensure that independent information exists to safeguard the well-being of affected communities.

Considerable contamination remains. On islands such as Bikini, the average background gamma radiation is double the maximum value stipulated by an agreement between the governments of the Marshall Islands and the U.S., even without taking into account other exposure pathways. Our findings, based on gathered data, run contrary to the DOE's. One conclusion is clear: absent a renewed effort to clean radiation from Bikini, families forced from their homes may not be able to safely return until the radiation naturally diminishes over decades and centuries.

Beyond plutonium and uranium, strontium 90 is a radioisotope of concern in the Marshall Islands. It can cause leukemia, bone cancer and bone marrow cancer and has long been a source of health concerns at nuclear disasters such as Chernobyl and Fukushima. Despite this, the U.S. government's published data don't speak to the presence of this dangerous nuclear isotope.

We have tested sediment from two bomb craters in the northern Marshall Islands and found consistently high values of strontium 90. Although detecting this radioisotope in sediment does not neatly translate into contamination in soil or food, the finding suggests the possibility of danger to ecosystems and people.

More than that, cleaning up strontium 90 and other contaminants in the Marshall Islands is possible. Congress should appropriate funds, and a research agency, such as the National Science Foundation, should initiate a call for proposals to fund independent research with three aims. We must first further understand the current radiological conditions across the Marshall Islands; second, explore new technologies and methods already in use for future cleanup activity; and, third, train Marshallese scientists, such as those working with the nation's National Nuclear Commission, to rebuild trust on this issue.

Through the collective work of dozens of researchers rather than a small group of scientists at the DOE, remediation efforts across the world will benefit. The Marshallese people and other affected communities have told us for decades just how dangerous nuclear weapons are. Let's heed their warnings before it is too late.

About the Authors

Hart Rapaport is a researcher at Columbia University's K=1 Project, Center for Nuclear Studies.

Ivana Nikolić Hughes is a senior lecturer in chemistry at Columbia University and the director of Frontiers of Science, a required course for Columbia College students. Ivana is also the director of the K=1 Project, Center for Nuclear Studies.

The Future of Nuclear Power: Let a Thousand Flowers Bloom

By Ashutosh Jogalekar

In the summer of 1956, a handful of men gathered in a former little red schoolhouse in San Diego. These men were among the most imaginative scientists and engineers of their generation. There was their leader, Frederic de Hoffmann who had worked on the Manhattan Project and was now the president of the company General Atomics. Hoffmann was not only a creative physicist but also an unusually shrewd and capable manager and entrepreneur; in the later years of his life he would take the celebrated Salk Institute to great heights. There was also Freeman Dyson, a remarkably versatile mathematical physicist from the Institute for Advanced Study in Princeton who had previously reconciled disparate theories of quantum electrodynamics–the strange theory of light and matter. And there was Edward Teller, another Manhattan Project veteran; a dark, volatile and brilliant physicist who would become so convinced of the power of nuclear weapons to save the world that he would inspire the caricature of the mad scientist in Stanley Kubrick's classic film *Dr. Strangelove*.

Together these men and their associates worked on a single goal: the creation of a nuclear reactor that was intrinsically safe, one that would cease and desist its nuclear transformations even in the face of human folly and stupidity. The reactor would have the rather uninspired name TRIGA (Training, Research, Isotopes, General Atomics) but its legacy would be anything but uninspiring. At the heart of the reactor's success was not a technical innovation but an open atmosphere of debate and discussion. Every day someone–mostly Teller–would come up with ten ideas, most of which sounded crazy. The others–mostly Dyson–would then patiently work through the ideas, discarding several of them, extracting the gems from the dross and giving them rigorous shape.

TRIGA benefited from a maximum of free inquiry and individual creativity and a minimum of bureaucratic interference. There was no overarching managerial body dictating the thoughts of the designers. Everyone was free to come up with any idea they thought of, and the job of the rest of the group was to either refine the idea and make it more rigorous and practical or discard it and move on to the next idea. The makers of TRIGA would have been right at home with the computer entrepreneurs of Silicon Valley a few decades later.

At the core of TRIGA's operation was a principle called the warm neutron principle. In a conventional reactor, the neutrons in the fuel are moderated by hydrogen in the cooler water from the surroundings. There is a significant potential for a meltdown if someone pulls out the control rods, since the water which stays cool for a while will continue to moderate the neutrons and sustain their efficacy for causing fission. Dyson and Teller's idea was to place half of the hydrogen in the water and the rest in the fuel in the form of a uranium and zirconium hydride alloy. This would result in only half of the hydrogen staying cool enough to moderate the neutrons, while the other half in the hydride stays warm and diminishes the ability of the neutrons to fission uranium. This results in the fuel having what is called a negative temperature coefficient. The fuel rods were fashioned with care and precision by Massoud Simnad, an Iranian metallurgist working on the project.

The warm neutron principle is what made TRIGA intrinsically safe, very unlikely to sustain a meltdown or catastrophic failure. It took less than three years for the engineers and technicians to take the reactor from the design stage to manufacturing. The first TRIGA was inaugurated by none other than Niels Bohr in San Diego. Seventy of these safe reactors were built. They were safe and cheap enough to be operated in hospitals and universities by students and their main function was to produce isotopes for scientific and engineering experiments. They were also robust and safe enough to be proliferation resistant. As Dyson recounts in his elegant memoir *Disturbing the Universe*, the TRIGA is perhaps the only nuclear reactor that made a profit for its creator.

TRIGA made the development of nuclear power seem relatively easy, cheap and fast. Why didn't other reactors enjoy the same success? Why, after fifty years, is nuclear power still struggling in the face of economics and political and social backlash? There are many reasons, but the principal reason is simple: the designers of TRIGA were encouraged to have fun and they had the kind of freedom of inquiry commonly found in a startup company. The problem is that the fun went out of the nuclear business in the 70s and with fun, creativity and cost considerations also went out of the window. In his book Dyson swiftly cuts through to the central issue:

> *The fundamental problem of the nuclear industry is not reactor safety, not waste disposal, not the dangers of nuclear proliferation, real though all these problems are. The fundamental problem of the industry is that nobody any longer has any fun building reactors. ... Sometime between 1960 and 1970 the fun went out of the business. The adventurers, the experimenters, the inventors, were driven out, and the accountants and managers took control. The accountants and managers decided that it was not cost effective to let bright people play with weird reactors. So the weird reactors disappeared and with them the chance of any radical improvement beyond our existing systems. We are left with a very small number of reactor types, each of them frozen into a huge bureaucratic organization, each of them in various ways technically unsatisfactory, each of them less safe than many possible alternative designs which have been discarded. Nobody builds reactors for fun anymore. The spirit of the little red schoolhouse is dead. That, in my opinion, is what went wrong with nuclear power.*

Nobody builds reactors for fun anymore. What Dyson is getting at is quite simple. For any technological development to be possible, the technology needs to drive itself with the fuel of Darwinian innovation. It needs to generate all possible ideas–including the weird ones–and then fish out the best while ruthlessly weeding out the worst. This leads not only to quality but cost reduction since no entrepreneur is going to risk introducing an inherently expensive technology into the market. But all this is not possible until you allow people to play with ideas of their own volition and have fun doing it. People are not going to selflessly generate ideas by fiat, they are only going to do so when they are supported by funds and infrastructure but otherwise left to their own devices. The accountants and managers need to get the process started and then need to get out of the way.

Almost every successful technology has gone through this Darwinian phase. Dyson gives the example of motorcycles, which motorcyclists from his father's generation designed and serviced with care and affection. In our generation the most resounding example is that of computer technology. We have lost track of how many versions of software and hardware young computer enthusiasts experimented with in their California garages before their own technical and artistic sensibilities and the will of the market picked the best ones. Both Bill Gates and Steve Jobs made their fortunes in a milieu of young upstarts experimenting with the latest electronics and code and competing with fellow upstarts sprawled across the country. Just like the nuclear designers of the little red schoolhouse, the computer designers of the Silicon Valley garages were unencumbered by the demands of a central authority. So were the genetic engineers who founded companies like Genentech and Amgen. They could let their imaginations roam, bouncing ideas off one another and ruthlessly shooting down clumsy, expensive or ostentatious designs. It was the ability of bright young people to brainstorm to their hearts' content and to launch nimble startups rapidly exploring diverse and cheap technological solutions that allowed computer technology to become the all-pervasive life force that it is today. Biotechnology is now poised to do the same. A similar process of Darwinian survival of the fittest permeates other successful technologies, from flight to automobile engineering to house construction. And most importantly, the creators of all these technologies had fun creating them.

Nothing like this happened with nuclear power. It was a technology whose development was dictated by a few prominent government and military officials and large organizations and straitjacketed within narrow constraints. Most of the developers of nuclear technologies were staid, elderly bureaucrats rather than young iconoclasts like Frederic de Hoffmann. An early design invented by Admiral Hyman Rickover–suitable for submarines but hardly optimal for efficient land-based power stations–was frozen and applied to hundreds of reactors around the country. Since then there have been only a hundred or so reactor designs and only half a dozen or so prominent ones. Due to a complicated mix of factors including public paranoia, lack of economies of scale, political correctness and misunderstandings about radiation, nuclear technology was never given a chance to be played around with, to be entrusted to youthful entrepreneurs experimenting with ideas, to find its own way through the creative and destructive process of Darwinian evolution to a plateau of technological and economic efficiency. The result was that the field remained both scientifically narrow and expensive. Even today there are only a handful of companies building and operating most of the world's reactors.

To reinvigorate the promise of nuclear power to provide cheap energy to the world and combat climate change, the field needs to be infused with the same entrepreneurial spirit that pervaded the TRIGA design team and the Silicon Valley entrepreneurs. Young people who are brimming with ideas especially need to be given as many resources as possible to come up with solutions and explore them in startups, even if not garages. Just like any other technology, nuclear power can thrive only when the maximum number of people apply their creative minds to improving both the quality and cost of energy from fission. Fortunately a minority of companies and their creators are setting the trends.

I live in Cambridge, MA which has been a hotbed of innovation for several decades. In a few square miles along the picturesque Charles River lie literally hundreds of biotech, pharmaceutical and information technology startups, most enabled by the proximity of MIT and Harvard whose laboratories provide a steady supply of ideas that can be potentially turned into useful products. The scientists, engineers and managers in these startups constantly compete against each other and between themselves for the best ideas. My own startup is based on a novel way to make complex drugs using the specific base-pairing properties of DNA. Every year dozens of startups fail, and a few go public or are bought by other companies. The whole startup enterprise in Cambridge is subject to the forces of Darwinian selection that enables the filtering of the best ideas.

One component of this enterprise is named Transatomic Power. It was started by a duo of graduate students from MIT named Leslie Dewan and Mark Massie in 2010. The goal of Transatomic Power is to design a reactor that can generate power from nuclear waste, thus addressing the twin issues of clean energy and nuclear waste removal at the same time. The reactor which is a molten salt reactor lives off the preponderance of energy trapped in unfissioned reactor fuel from light water reactors. It is also compact enough to be shipped individually to the reactor site. Dewan and Massie are two of the few young people who actually see opportunity in the nuclear field and are willing to take risks in order to develop a novel approach to the problem.

On the other coast of the United States in Seattle is another team of nuclear entrepreneurs led by Nathan Myhrvold, a former CTO of Microsoft with degrees in physics and economics. Myhrvold has founded a company named Terrapower which operates on a novel nuclear design called the traveling wave reactor (TWR) which was also in part explored by Edward Teller and Lowell Wood in the 90s. The TWR is another reactor which can operate on waste, using depleted uranium to sustain a fission wave that spreads outward into the reactor, transforming the uranium into plutonium and leaving a small amount of fissile waste behind. The TWR promises to run for decades without having to refuel it or recover spent fuel, thus promising both safety and proliferation resistance. Among the enthusiasts of the TWR is Bill Gates, who knows a thing or two about Darwinian innovation in technology.

The founders of Terrapower and Transatomic are following in the footsteps of the dreamers in the little red schoolhouse. They have transformed nuclear technology into an entrepreneurial game of ideas and funding sustained by a healthy interplay between academic, industrial and government laboratories. I do not know whether their reactors will be the ones supplying the world's energy in the near future, but what I do know is that they are doing exactly what needs to be done to sustain the innovative process of creation and destruction that is necessary for the evolution of any successful technology. They are bucking the trend set by the large, bureaucratic government organizations and their industrial counterparts. And most importantly, they are having fun doing it, trading ideas and exploring new technical ground. I see hope in the adventures of these nuclear explorers, just like the makers of TRIGA saw hope in the future of nuclear power and the whole world saw hope in the explorers of computer and biotechnology in the 80s. When it comes to nuclear technology, we should let a thousand flowers bloom. And then we can pick the most beautiful.

This article was published in Scientific American*'s former blog network and reflects the views of the author, not necessarily those of* Scientific American.

About the Author

Ashutosh Jogalekar is a chemist interested in the history, philosophy and sociology of science. He is fascinated by the logic of scientific discovery and by the interaction of science with public sentiments and policy. He blogs at The Curious Wavefunction and can be reached at curiouswavefunction@gmail.com.

Section 2: New Types of Power Plants

First U.S. Small Nuclear Reactor Design Is Approved

By Dave Levitan; edited by Mark Fischetti

The U.S. Nuclear Regulatory Commission (NRC) has approved the design of a new kind of reactor, known as a small modular reactor (SMR). The design, from the Portland, Ore.–based company NuScale Power, is intended to speed construction, lower cost and improve safety over traditional nuclear reactors, which are typically many times larger. Supporters of SMRs have long touted them as a way to help revive the country's nuclear industry and widen the spread of low-carbon electricity. But some experts have expressed concerns over the potential expense and remaining safety issues that the industry would have to address before any such reactors are actually built.

"This is a significant milestone not only for NuScale, but also for the entire U.S. nuclear sector," said NuScale chairman and CEO John Hopkins in a press release.

The NRC's design approval and related final safety evaluation report (FSER) do not mean that the firm can begin constructing reactors. But utility companies can now apply to the NRC to build and operate NuScale's design. With almost no new nuclear construction completed in the U.S. over the past three decades, SMRs could help reinvigorate a flagging industry.

NuScale's SMR, developed with the help of almost $300 million from the U.S. Department of Energy, has a generating capacity of 50 megawatts—substantially smaller than standard nuclear reactors, which can range to well more than 1,000 megawatts (MW). A utility could combine up to 12 SMRs at a single site, producing 600 MW of electricity—enough to power a midsize city. The NRC says it expects an application for a 60-MW version of NuScale's SMR in 2022.

The nuclear industry says SMRs could be built much faster and cheaper than conventional reactors—like products that are rolled off a production line and shipped to various locations rather than custom-built at each site. A customer could also order and combine various numbers of units, making a wide range of capacity possible. According to the International Atomic Energy Agency, dozens of SMR designs are under consideration around the world, and several are in "advanced stages of construction" in Argentina, China and Russia.

Some industry proponents argue that SMRs are the best option for bringing large amounts of emissions-free technology online in the short term to help battle climate change. Opponents have cited the unresolved issue of disposing nuclear waste, as well as the significant price tag and time involved in building any nuclear plant, compared with renewable energy sources.

NuScale believes it can avoid the dramatic cost overruns and years-long delays that have plagued construction of traditional nuclear power plants in recent decades. Diane Hughes, the company's vice president of marketing and communications, says that the company expects to sell anywhere from 674 to 1,682 reactors between 2023 and 2042. The high end of that range would represent more than 80 gigawatts of capacity, which approaches the 98 gigawatts of existing nuclear capacity in the U.S. That power is supplied by just under 100 large reactors; the existing plants provide approximately 20 percent of the country's electricity. NuScale has signed memorandums of understanding with companies and utilities in the U.S., Canada, Jordan, Romania, Ukraine and other countries. The agreements simply mean the parties will jointly explore potential deals.

NuScale's first scheduled project is with Utah Associated Municipal Power Systems (UAMPS), a state-based organization that supplies wholesale electricity to small, community-owned utilities in surrounding states. NuScale plans to deliver its first reactor to the UAMPS project at the Idaho National Laboratory by 2027; it is scheduled to be operational by 2029. Another 11 reactors will round out the 720-MW project by 2030. A portion of the generated power will be sold to the U.S. Department of Energy, with the rest purchased by UAMPS member utilities. Agreements for some of the power are in place, although a few municipalities have already walked away because of price concerns. Others have until September 30 to exit the project.

Experts have expressed skepticism about both the safety of the NuScale SMR and its potential costs. In an online press event on September 2, M. V. Ramana, a professor and nuclear expert at the University of British Columbia, discussed a report he prepared at the request of Oregon Physicians for Social Responsibility that highlighted significant issues associated with the UAMPS project.

"I am sorry to say that what lies ahead is risky and expensive," Ramana said. Just in the past five years, he noted, cost estimates from various sources for the UAMPS project have risen from approximately $3 billion to more than $6 billion. NuScale's initial goal of having operational reactors by 2016 has been extended by more than a decade, reflecting the sluggish U.S. nuclear industry in general. Costs to consumers could far exceed those associated with other emissions-free power sources such as solar and wind, Ramana added.

And despite the NRC's design approval of the new SMR, some safety features still require adjustment. "I don't think future NuScale applicants will benefit from a design certification that has safety gaps in it," says Edwin Lyman, director of nuclear power safety at the Union of Concerned Scientists. He points out that the NRC has issued its final safety report in spite of questions raised both by an expert at the agency and an external advisory board.

In a July 2020 report, NRC nuclear engineer Shanlai Lu discussed a complicated issue known as boron dilution, which could possibly cause "fuel failure and prompt criticality condition"–meaning that even if a reactor is shut down, fission reactions could restart and begin a dangerous power increase. And in another report, the NRC's Advisory Committee on Reactor Safeguards also noted that "several potentially risk-significant items" are not yet completed, though it did still recommend that the NRC issue the FSER. The agency's response to the latter report stated that those items will be further assessed when site-specific licensing applications–the step needed to actually begin building and operating a reactor–are submitted.

"NuScale and the U.S. Nuclear Regulatory Commission staff examined boron dilution in great detail and reached similar conclusions that the NuScale small modular reactor design is safe and meets all requirements, as is affirmed by the NRC's recent issuance of the FSER," NuScale's Hughes says.

Lyman says that in general, the NRC's design certification process should reduce uncertainty for utilities aiming to build nuclear plants because they can reference a completed safety review. But he thinks the NuScale approval undermines that advantage. Whether the gaps in safety will result in further delays to NuScale's time line remains to be seen. The NRC will undertake another review when the company's 60-MW design is submitted.

So-Called Next-Generation Nuclear Power Plants Are Being Oversold

By Elliott Negin

The U.S. nuclear power industry is at an impasse. Since 2012, 11 of the 104 light-water reactors in operation at the time have closed, mainly as a result of aging infrastructure and the inability to compete with natural gas, wind and solar, which are now the cheapest sources of electricity in the U.S. and most other countries worldwide.

One way the industry is trying to reverse the trend is by looking to what it likes to call "advanced" reactors. Despite the name, these designs are largely based on unproven concepts from more than 50 years ago. Unlike conventional light-water reactors, these rely on sodium or molten salt or gas for cooling, and their proponents claim they will be less expensive, safer and more secure than their predecessors. Some claim that these innovative devices will be ready for prime time by the end of this decade.

This has naturally attracted the attention of Biden administration officials and some key members of Congress, who are looking for ways to curb carbon emissions. But an analysis of non-light-water reactor concepts in development by the Union of Concerned Scientists (UCS) has found that these designs are no better–and in some respects significantly worse–than the light-water reactors in operation today. The report's author, UCS physicist Edwin Lyman, took a close look at the claims developers have been making: that these new devices will burn uranium fuel more efficiently and produce less radioactive waste than existing plants; will reduce the risk of nuclear proliferation; and will be commercialized relatively soon. Those claims, however, do not hold up to scrutiny.

One contender, for example, TerraPower's 345-megawatt Natrium reactor, received considerable media attention earlier this year when company founder Bill Gates touted it during interviews about his new book, *How to Avoid a Climate Disaster*. According to the UCS report, however, sodium-cooled fast reactors such as Natrium would likely be less uranium-efficient and would not reduce the amount of waste that requires long-term isolation. They could also experience safety problems that are not an issue for light-water reactors. Sodium coolant, for instance, can burn when exposed to air or water, and the Natrium's design could experience uncontrollable power increases that result in rapid core melting.

In June, TerraPower announced that it would build the first Natrium reactor in Wyoming as part of a 50–50 cost-share program with the Department of Energy. The DOE program originally required the company to have the reactor, still in its early design stage, up and running by 2027. That was recently pushed back a year, but it is still a completely unrealistic timetable. According to the UCS report, if federal regulators require the necessary safety demonstrations, it could take at least 20 years–and billions of dollars in additional costs–to commercialize such reactors, their associated fuel-cycle facilities, and other related infrastructure.

The Nuclear Regulatory Commission (NRC) may have to adapt some regulations when licensing reactor technologies that differ significantly in design from the current fleet. Lyman says that should not mean weakening public health and safety standards, finding no justification for the claim that "advanced" reactors will be so much safer and more secure that the NRC can exempt them from fundamental safeguards. On the contrary, because there are so many open questions about these reactors, he says they may need to meet even more stringent requirements.

Lyman's report recommends that the DOE suspend its advanced reactor demonstration program until the NRC determines whether it will require full-scale prototype tests before any designs are licensed for commercial deployment, which the report argues are essential. It also calls on Congress to require the NRC to convene an independent commission to review the technical merits of non-light-water reactors and approve only those projects that have a high likelihood of commercialization and are clearly safer and more secure than the current fleet.

Finally, it recommends that the NRC and Congress consider spending more research and development dollars on improving the safety and security of light-water reactors rather than on commercializing immature, overhyped non-light-water reactor designs. Any federal appropriations for R&D and deployment of these reactor designs, Lyman says, should be guided by a realistic assessment of the likely benefits and not based on wishful thinking.

About the Author

Elliott Negin is a senior writer at the Union of Concerned Scientists.

What Is the Future of Fusion Energy?

By Philip Ball

Last December physicists working on fusion claimed a breakthrough. A team at the National Ignition Facility (NIF) in California announced it had extracted more energy from a controlled nuclear fusion reaction than had been used to trigger it. It was a global first and a significant step for physics–but very far from enabling practical exploitation of fusion as an energy source. The high-profile announcement elicited a familiar pattern of responses to fusion research: acclaim from boosters of the technology and dismissals from skeptics, who complain that scientists continually promise that fusion is just 20 years away (or 30 or 50, take your pick).

These fervent reactions reflect the high stakes for fusion. The world is increasingly desperate for an abundant source of clean energy that can mitigate the climate crisis created by burning fossil fuels. Nuclear fusion–the merging of light atomic nuclei–has the potential to produce energy with near-zero carbon emissions, without creating the dangerous radioactive waste associated with today's nuclear fission reactors, which split the very heavy nuclei of radioactive elements. Physicists have been studying fusion power since the 1950s, but turning it into a practical energy source has remained frustratingly elusive. Will it ever be a significant source of power for our energy-hungry planet–and if so, will it arrive in time to save Earth from meltdown?

The latter question is one of the few in this field to which there is a clear answer. Most experts agree that we're unlikely to be able to generate large-scale energy from nuclear fusion before around 2050 (the cautious might add on another decade). Given that the global temperature rise over the current century may be largely determined by what we do–or fail to do–about carbon emissions before then, fusion can be no savior. "I do think fusion looks a lot more plausible now than it did 10 years ago as a future energy source," says Omar Hurricane, a program leader at Lawrence Livermore National Laboratory, where the NIF is housed. "But it's not going to be viable in the next 10 to 20 years, so we need other solutions."

Decarbonizing by mid-century will therefore depend on other technologies: renewables such as solar and wind; nuclear fission; and perhaps carbon-capture techniques. As we look further out, though, there are good reasons to think fusion will be a key part of the energy economy in the second half of the century, when more developing countries will start requiring Western-size energy budgets. And solving the problem of climate change is not a one-time affair. If we can navigate the bottleneck of the next few decades without transforming the climate too radically, the road beyond may be smoother.

The Long Haul

Nuclear fusion was recognized as a potential source of energy almost as soon as fission was. In a debriefing meeting of the Manhattan Project in late 1945, Italian physicist Enrico Fermi, who led the project to build the first fission reactor in Chicago during World War II, envisioned fusion reactors for power generation. Scientists figured out how to release fusion energy a few years later but only in the uncontrolled Armageddon-like explosions of hydrogen bombs. Once we learned how to conduct the process in a controlled and sustained manner, some scientists predicted, electricity would become "too cheap to meter."

But the challenges proved much greater than expected. "It's superhard," Hurricane says. "We're basically making stars on Earth." The fusion of two hydrogen atoms to make helium is the main process that powers the sun and other stars. When such light atomic nuclei combine, they release an immense amount of energy. But because these nuclei have positive electrical charges, they repel one another, and it takes tremendous pressures and temperatures to overcome that electrostatic barrier and get them to merge. If scientists can contain the fuel for fusion—a plasma mixture of deuterium and tritium, two heavy isotopes of hydrogen—the energy released in the reaction can make it self-sustaining. But how do you bottle a plasma at a temperature of around 100 million kelvins, several times hotter than the center of the sun?

No known material can withstand such extreme conditions; they would melt even extremely heat-resistant metals such as tungsten in an instant. The answer long favored for reactor design is magnetic confinement: holding the electrically charged plasma in a "magnetic bottle" formed by strong magnetic fields so it never touches the walls of the fusion chamber. The most popular design, called a tokamak and proposed in the 1950s by Soviet scientists, uses a toroidal (or doughnut-shaped) container.

The process requires exquisite control. The furiously hot plasma won't stay still: it tends to develop large temperature gradients, which generate strong convection currents that make the plasma turbulent and hard to manage. Such instabilities, akin to miniature solar flares, can bring the plasma into contact with the walls, damaging them. Other plasma instabilities can produce beams of high-energy electrons that bore holes in the reaction-chamber cladding. Suppressing or managing these fluctuations has been one of the key challenges for tokamak designers. "The big success of the past 10 years has been in understanding this turbulence in quantitative detail," says Steven Cowley, who directs the Princeton Plasma Physics Laboratory.

One of the biggest obstacles to magnetic-confinement fusion is the need for materials that can withstand the tough treatment they'll receive from the fusing plasma. In particular, deuterium-tritium fusion makes an intense flux of high-energy neutrons, which collide with the nuclei of atoms in the metal walls and cladding, causing tiny spots of melting. The metal then recrystallizes but is weakened, with atoms shifted from their initial positions. In the cladding of a typical fusion reactor, each atom might be displaced about 100 times over the reactor's lifetime.

The consequences of such intense neutron bombardment aren't well understood, because fusion has never been sustained for the long periods that would be required in a working reactor. "We don't know and won't know about materials degradation and lifetime until we've operated a power plant," says Ian Chapman, CEO of the U.K. Atomic

Energy Authority (UKAEA), the British government's nuclear energy organization. Nevertheless, important insights into these degradation problems might be gleaned from a simple experiment that generates intense neutron beams that can be used to test materials. Such a facility—a particle-accelerator-based project called the International Fusion Materials Irradiation Facility–Demo Oriented Neutron Source—should begin operating in Granada, Spain, in the early 2030s. A similar U.S. facility called the Fusion Prototypic Neutron Source has been proposed but doesn't yet have approval.

There is still no guarantee that these material issues can be solved. If they prove insurmountable, one alternative is to make the reactor walls from liquid metal, which can't be damaged by melting and recrystallization. But that, Cowley says, brings in a whole suite of other technical concerns.

Another major challenge is making the fusion fuel. The world has abundant deuterium: this isotope constitutes 0.016 percent of natural hydrogen, so the seas are literally awash in it. But tritium forms only in small quantities naturally, and it decays radioactively with a half-life of just 12 years, so it's constantly disappearing and must be produced afresh. In principle, it can be "bred" from fusion reactions because the fusion neutrons will react with lithium to make it. Most reactor designs incorporate this breeding process by surrounding the reactor chamber with a blanket of lithium. All the same, the technology is unproven at large scales, and no one really knows whether or how well tritium production and extraction will work.

Gargantuan Machines

The largest fusion project in the world, ITER (Latin for "the way" and originally an acronym for "International Thermonuclear Experimental Reactor") in southern France, will use a massive tokamak with a plasma radius of 6.2 meters; the entire machine will weigh 23,000 metric tons. If all goes to plan, ITER—supported by the European Union, the U.K., China, India, Japan, South Korea, Russia and the U.S.—will be the first fusion reactor to demonstrate continuous energy output at the scale of a power plant (about 500 megawatts, or MW). Construction began in 2007. The initial hope was that plasmas would be produced in the fusion chamber by about 2020, but ITER has suffered repeated delays while the estimated cost of $5.45 billion has quadrupled. This past January the project's leaders announced a further setback: the intended start of operation in 2035 may be delayed to the 2040s. ITER will not produce commercial power–as its name says, it is strictly an experimental machine intended to resolve engineering problems and prepare the way for viable power plants.

This new holdup of what some regard as a cumbersome behemoth with no guarantee of success prompted another bout of fusion skepticism. But such problems are to be expected, Hurricane says. "ITER is getting beaten up a lot, but we need to give them a break and let them sort out the problems," he says.

Chapman agrees. "It was very predictable that there would be problems, both politically and technically," he says. "The project is doing amazing things, including establishing supply chains that didn't exist before." The delay is disappointing, he admits, "but I don't think we'll look back on ITER and think it was a mistake. We'll think it was really important in the genesis of fusion. I'm convinced it will work."

Tokamaks for power plants will probably not need to be as gargantuan, and certainly cannot be as expensive, as ITER. Lately there has been increasing interest in smaller devices with a more spherical shape, like a cored apple. One of these, called the Spherical Tokamak for Energy Production (STEP), is being planned by the UKAEA as a pilot plant to be developed in parallel with ITER.

The spherical design concept had a successful proof-of-principle run with a device called the Mega Ampere Spherical Tokamak (MAST), which operated from 1999 to 2013, overseen by UKAEA and the European Atomic Energy Community (Euratom). These smaller machines have a higher energy density and thus a greater risk of heat damage, especially from the extraction of hot spent fuel in the "exhaust" system. An improved version–MAST Upgrade–turned on in 2020 and has been able to extract heat about 20 times more efficiently than the original. "That really does open the path to conceiving of a compact power plant," Chapman says.

Enter STEP, which aims to be just that: a prototype plant that produces net electricity. It is still in the concept design phase, but already the U.K. government has moved to create bespoke regulation for the project–the first in the world for fusion–that eliminates the need for a conventional nuclear license. Leaders selected a site last October: a coal power station in northern England that ceased operating in March and is scheduled to be demolished in early 2024. The site already has a cooling water supply and connections to the national grid and railway system.

The E.U. is planning its own prototype plant, called the DEMOnstration Power Plant (DEMO), administered by the EUROfusion consortium and aiming to produce between 200 and 500 MW of electric power. Construction might begin in the early 2040s, says Tony Donné, EUROfusion's program manager. "I'm convinced we can build such a device in 10 years."

Donné adds that there are equivalent "stepping stone" projects toward fusion plants in South Korea, Japan and China; the U.S. made plans for a smaller device called the Fusion Nuclear Science Facility. "China has come to the party a bit late but is now investing heavily and growing its workforce rapidly," Chapman says. "It is definitely catching up with what already exists in Europe and the U.S." Donné believes that some friendly competition–a kind of "moon race" for the first prototype fusion plant–could be beneficial as long as countries continue to share information.

The Start-up Scene

It's not all about big national and international projects. Small spherical tokamaks are one of the technologies that have brought fusion within the reach of private companies. Several dozen fusion start-ups have sprung up around the world, such as Commonwealth

Fusion Systems (CFS) in Massachusetts, General Fusion in Canada, and Tokamak Energy in the U.K.

General Fusion, with support from the UKAEA, has just begun building a demonstration plant that it hopes (ambitiously) to have running by 2025. According to the company's former CEO Christofer Mowry, it will be "the first power-plant-relevant large-scale demonstration." Meanwhile CFS, in partnership with the Plasma Science and Fusion Center (PSFC) of the Massachusetts Institute of Technology and others, is building a prototype device called SPARC, also targeted for completion in 2025. SPARC will be a midsize tokamak in which the plasma is tightly confined by very intense magnetic fields produced by new high-temperature superconducting magnets developed at M.I.T. and unveiled in 2021. Such magnets were hailed as a significant step for magnetic-confinement fusion because the power density in the plasma increases rapidly as the strength of the magnetic field rises.

The SPARC team aims to extract net energy from the plasma (about 10 times more energy out than in) and to generate 50 to 140 MW of fusion power. Although SPARC is much smaller than ITER, the PSFC's director, Dennis Whyte, says its mission is similar: to solve the science and technology problems that stand in the way of commercialization. It won't feed any energy into the grid, but it's meant to clear a path for the "affordable, robust, compact" fusion reactor concept developed at M.I.T. and pursued by CFS, which Cowley considers "the most impactful company" so far.

Cowley welcomes such projects but cautions against seeing them as a shortcut to making fusion a realistic energy source. "We see these start-up companies coming in with a lot of enthusiasm, and a lot of their focus is on a particular part of the problem," he says. It's highly unlikely that one of them will make fusion energy commercial before the big guns, and many will simply fold–as some start-ups always do. But Chapman believes others will become valuable suppliers of expertise and of specialized components such as magnets. "Most of the small fusion companies will end up being part of the supply chain," he says.

Different Designs

Setups for magnetic-confinement fusion are not necessarily limited to tokamaks. In the 1950s astrophysicist Lyman Spitzer argued that plasma might be contained more effectively in a doughnut chamber with a twisted tunnel wall. With this configuration, the device could keep the plasma constrained by using the magnetic fields generated by flows in the charged plasma itself.

The more complex geometry of this design, called a stellarator, is tricky to engineer, but a few projects are pursuing it. A notable example is the Wendelstein 7-X stellarator in Greifswald, Germany, completed in 2015 and now operating again after a three-year upgrade. "A stellarator has some advantages, but technically it's a more complicated device," Donné says. "In Europe, we're working on the stellarator as a backup to the tokamak." The technology is still at a relatively early stage, so if that backup turns out to be essential, the timescale for practical fusion is likely to be pushed back again.

The strategy at the NIF is totally different from all of these projects. Instead of using a large amount of plasma confined by magnetic fields, the NIF experiment ignites a tiny target of deuterium and tritium. In this case, the fusing plasma is held in place only fleetingly by its own inertia after the experiment triggers fusion by squeezing the fuel abruptly and heating it intensely–a scheme called inertial confinement fusion. The NIF produces these extreme conditions by focusing very intense laser beams on the pellet-shaped targets. The fusion energy is released in a brief burst before the hot plasma expands. This kind of energy production would therefore happen in pulses, and fuel capsules would have to be constantly moved one after another into the reaction chamber to be ignited. Most researchers estimate that for the approach to be practical, capsules would have to be replaced about 10 times a second.

The challenges for inertial confinement fusion are daunting, and at present only a few facilities in the world are studying it. Besides the NIF, the biggest, there are the Megajoule Laser facility in France and the Shenguang-III laser facility in China; Russia also might be pursuing this approach, but the details are hard to ascertain. Energy generation isn't actually a main part of the NIF mission; the facility was intended mostly to trigger nuclear reactions for studying and maintaining the U.S. stockpile of nuclear weapons. "The primary work at the NIF has been funded entirely by the U.S. national security apparatus," Hurricane says. "It is not a fusion reactor and is not meant to demonstrate fusion energy in any practical sense."

Much more work lies ahead to make inertial confinement fusion a true contender for supplying energy. "The work has focused on the fundamental science, and we haven't put as much effort into the supporting technologies needed for a power plant," says Tammy Ma, who leads the NIF's inertial fusion energy initiative.

Looking Forward

Given this varied landscape of fusion projects, how close is practical fusion energy really? Chapman is blunt: "There is not today a single project underway to build a fusion power plant that will produce energy."

And real power plants—ones that aren't just prototypes—take a decade or so to construct. "Experiments are making progress, and the progress is impressive," Chapman says, "but fusion is not going to be working [as a source of mass energy] in a few years' time." Donné is blunter still: "Anyone who tells me that they'll have a working future reactor in five or 10 years is either completely ignorant or a liar."

Forecasting when fusion energy will arrive has always been a risky business, but experts now mostly agree on the approximate timescales. "Suppose we get a pilot plant that works by the end of the 2030s, although that would be going some," Cowley says. Such a plant is unlikely to be a blueprint for commercialization, and so, he says, "I think you'd have another stage of about 10 years from a pilot plant to the first commercial reactor." Chapman concurs that fusion plants might be feeding power into the grid by around

2050 and then could become steadily more important to the energy economy in the second half of the century, especially post-2060.

Fusion plants are likely to be of about the same scale as today's fossil-fuel or fission plants, with outputs of a few gigawatts. That means they could be constructed on the same sites, replacing like with like, and with all the necessary electrical-grid infrastructure already in place. "You could say that fusion is very easy to plug in and replace either fossil fuels or fission," Donné says. "This can be a very smooth transition." He expects that fusion plants will replace first the still active coal plants, then oil and gas, and finally fission.

Even if fusion can't save us from the immediate climate crisis, over the long term it may be the best option to satisfy our energy needs without destroying the planet. Soviet fusion visionary Lev Artsimovich, the "father of the tokamak," once said that the world will have nuclear fusion when it decides it needs it. "When we realize what climate change will do as an existential threat, the delivery of fusion will accelerate enormously," Chapman says, drawing an analogy to the quick development of COVID-19 vaccines. At the moment we simply have no other long-term way of getting to net-zero carbon emissions, especially because the global energy demand is projected to triple between 2050 and 2100. "Fusion is essential" to meet that need, Chapman says. "I can't see what else it will be." Renewables such as wind and solar energy definitely have a role to play, Donné says, but they aren't likely to be enough.

Building a new kind of energy infrastructure from the ground up presents opportunities as well as challenges. Nuclear fission planners made some serious mistakes in terms of design and public relations, but now the nascent fusion industry has a chance to learn from those mistakes and do better—not least by thinking about issues of energy equity and justice. "When we have these plants, where do we place them so that we can provide a clean energy source for all types of communities?" the NIF's Ma asks. "How do we build up a workforce that is diverse? How do we ensure that as we are building up this industry, we are training folks to have the skills of the future? We get to at least try to do it right this time."

About the Author

Philip Ball is a science writer and author based in London. His latest book is How Life Works *(University of Chicago Press, 2023).*

World's Largest Fusion Project Is in Big Trouble, New Documents Reveal

By Charles Seife; edited by Lee Billings

It could be a new world record, although no one involved wants to talk about it. In the south of France, a collaboration among 35 countries has been birthing one of the largest and most ambitious scientific experiments ever conceived: the giant fusion power machine known as the International Thermonuclear Experimental Reactor (ITER). But the only record ITER seems certain to set doesn't involve "burning" plasma at temperatures 10 times higher than that of the sun's core, keeping this "artificial star" ablaze and generating net energy for seconds at a time or any of fusion energy's other spectacular and myriad prerequisites. Instead ITER is on the verge of a record-setting disaster as accumulated schedule slips and budget overruns threaten to make it the most delayed–and most cost-inflated–science project in history.

ITER is supposed to help humanity achieve the dream of a world powered not by fossil fuels but by fusion energy, the same process that makes the stars shine. Conceived in the mid-1980s, the machine, when completed, will essentially be a giant, high-tech, doughnut-shaped vessel–known as a tokamak–that will contain hydrogen raised to such high temperatures that it will become ionized, forming a plasma rather than a gas. Powerful magnetic and electric fields flowing from and through the tokamak will girdle and heat the plasma cloud so that the atoms inside will collide and fuse together, releasing immense amounts of energy. But this feat is easier said than done. Since the 1950s fusion machines have grown bigger and more powerful, but none has ever gotten anywhere near what would be needed to put this panacea energy source on the electric grid. ITER is the biggest, most powerful fusion device ever devised, and its designers have intended it to be the machine that will finally show that fusion power plants can really be built.

The ITER project formally began in 2006, when its international partners agreed to fund an estimated €5 billion (then $6.3 billion), 10-year plan that would have seen ITER come online in 2016. The most recent official cost estimate stands at more than €20 billion ($22 billion), with ITER nominally turning on scarcely two years from now. Documents recently obtained via a lawsuit, however, imply that these figures are woefully outdated: ITER is not just facing several years' worth of additional delays but also a growing internal recognition that the project's remaining technical challenges are poised to send budgets spiraling even further out of control and successful operation ever further into the future.

The documents, drafted a year ago for a private meeting of the ITER Council, ITER's governing body, show that at the time, the project was bracing for a three-year delay–a doubling of internal estimates prepared just six months earlier. And in the year since those documents were written, the already grim news out of ITER has unfortunately only gotten worse. Yet no one within the ITER Organization has been able to provide estimates of the additional delays, much less the extra expenses expected to result from them. Nor has anyone at the U.S. Department of Energy, which is in charge of the nation's contributions to ITER, been able to do so. When contacted for this story, DOE officials did not respond to any questions by the time of publication.

The problems leading to these latest projected delays were several years in the making. The ITER Organization was extremely slow to let on that anything was wrong, however. As late as early July 2022, ITER's website announced that the machine was expected to turn on as scheduled in December 2025. Afterward that date bore an asterisk clarifying that it would be revised. Now the date has disappeared from the website altogether. ITER leaders seldom let slip that anything was awry either. In February 2017 ITER's then director general, the late Bernard Bigot, discussed its progress with DOE representatives. "ITER is really moving forward," he said. "We are working day and night. ...The progress is on schedule." The timeline he presented implied that everything was on track. Construction of the ITER complex's foundation, which incorporates an earthquake protection system with hundreds of tremor-dampening rubber- and metal-laminated plates, should have been almost complete. From there, assembly of the reactor itself was planned to begin in 2018. At the time of Bigot's remarks, two of its major pieces—a massive magnetic coil to wrap around the doughnutlike tokamak and a large section of the vacuum vessel that makes up the tokamak's walls—were supposed to be ready to ship within the month and by the end of the year, respectively. Instead the coil would take almost three more years to complete, as would the vessel sector. The pieces were completed in January and April 2020, respectively. In fact, a large proportion of the big components of the machine were behind schedule by a year or two years or even more. Soon ITER's official start of assembly was bumped from 2018 to 2020.

Then, in early 2020, the COVID pandemic struck, slowing manufacturing and shipping of machine components.

In late 2021 the ITER Council quietly asked for a revised schedule and estimate of costs, which was eventually presented at a closed meeting in June 2022—almost precisely a month after Bigot died from an unspecified illness. Some months later, when I asked Laban Coblentz, ITER's head of communications, what exactly that revised schedule was, like everyone else on the project, he refused to disclose this information—or any other hint of how grave the delays or cost overruns were likely to be. According to Coblentz, Bigot's death had pushed ITER into a "rather traumatic transition in leadership" that effectively rendered the revised schedule moot. There wasn't, he said, "any relevance to providing you with an internal document, circulated to the ITER Council in June [2022], which is no longer current or in any sense accurate."

In response to this stonewalling, earlier this year I initiated a lawsuit under the U.S. Freedom of Information Act seeking to reveal the extent of ITER's expected schedule and cost troubles. So far, the lawsuit has been partially successful. It has extracted partially redacted documents revealing that in November 2021 ITER's internal estimates showed the project already facing about 17 months of delays. By the time of the June 2022 ITER Council meeting, the number had doubled to roughly 35 months of delays—enough to easily add billions of dollars to ITER's already bloated budget. But this timeline didn't reflect other events bound to introduce even more delays.

In addition to some of ITER's components arriving far behind schedule, some of that machinery also turned out to be defective. Several thermal shields meant to keep ITER's liquid helium refrigerant cold and protect the walls of the machine corroded and cracked because of the way the welds interacted with an acid used to wash the metal. This needs to be repaired. "So all in all, it's removing about 20 kilometers of very thin piping, replacing that—in most cases, repairing the thermal shields, in some cases, making new ones," Coblentz says. "That is not a high-cost component in ITER terms." In addition, some of the puzzle-piece-like parts of the vacuum vessel—intended to fit together with submillimeter precision—proved not to be manufactured as precisely as needed. "You can call that a manufacturing flaw, legitimately," Coblentz adds. In November 2022 the ITER Organization decided not only to halt assembly of the vacuum vessel but also to remove the already installed segment for repairs. Even so, Kathryn McCarthy, director of the U.S. ITER Project at Oak Ridge National Laboratory, testified to Congress just this week that ITER's "continued project progress shows us that it is possible to achieve engineering precision, at the millimeter-scale, on ship-sized fusion components."

On top of that difficulty, in January 2022 the French Nuclear Safety Authority (ASN) put a stop to ITER assembly entirely. ASN is unconvinced that, among other issues, the planned amount of radiation shielding around the machine will be adequate, and the authority won't let the assembly go forward until ITER can prove that it can keep personnel safe. But adding much more shielding might pile on more weight than the rubber-and-metal earthquake-resistant foundation can bear. "ASN will reconsider lifting the tokamak assembly hold point on the basis of a self-supported dossier [ASN] requested from the ITER organization," wrote ASN spokesperson Evangelia Petit in an e-mail to me. This dossier must address, among other things, biological protection against radiation hazards. Coblentz, however, says the impasse has been caused by "excessive conservatism" and suggests that the situation might be resolved by allowing ITER to run at low power so that the radiation hazard can be mapped and understood more fully before switching over to high-power operations.

In late 2022 Bigot's replacement, Pietro Barabaschi, admitted that the problem with the vacuum vessel and thermal blankets would wreak havoc on the timing of ITER's much vaunted initial run, its so-called first plasma date. "We are of course very much aware of the consequences as far as schedule and cost are concerned–and they will not be insignificant," he said in a November 2022 ITER press release. The length and cost of those delays are still unclear, however, and Barabaschi's statement didn't address the supply chain issues–or the regulatory ones, which have not improved. In March 2023 ASN found that the qualifications of certain welders–who have to make nuclear-plant-grade welds between metal parts–had been falsified. ITER officials subsequently banned the vendor that supplied the welding services from any activity on the worksite, but ASN required ITER to go through all the relevant contractor contributions and prepare an impact statement about the falsifications. Coblentz believes that an approximately three-year delay caused by late components and supply chain issues discussed in 2022 and a roughly two-year delay caused by the defective vacuum vessel segments and thermal blankets won't be additive–that many of the problems can be worked out in parallel. In fact, he says, the ITER organization will possibly start installing equipment not needed until after the first plasma date–a date, he suggests, that might not even be a relevant goalpost anymore.

Whether the wait slips four or five or even more years, ITER is far from the only big scientific project to face enormous delays, cost growth and moving goalposts. Such obstacles, its advocates say, are unavoidable when attempting ambitious tasks that require large amounts of technological development. Proponents of megaproject largesse may cite the James Webb Space Telescope (JWST) as an apt example: intended to be completed in a decade at a cost of a bit more than $1 billion, it took 20 years and more than $10 billion to get the telescope off the ground. Those overruns were especially painful for astronomers but in hindsight seem justified, given that they ensured JWST's successful launch, deployment and ongoing revolutionary observations in deep space.

But ITER and JWST are not remotely the same. ITER's gestation has been even longer—stretching back to a handshake agreement between Ronald Reagan and Mikhail Gorbachev in the mid-1980s—and its cost is higher than any scientific endeavor in history. Adjusted for inflation, its price is about the same as that of the Manhattan Project, which made the first atomic bombs—and is almost certain to get larger. As early as 2018 the DOE's undersecretary for science told Congress that the machine was going to cost much more than the then official price tag of $22 billion. ITER officials vigorously disputed this claim, but the as-yet-undisclosed effects of the project's latest setbacks makes it clear, at least, that the final bill will be billions more still.

And unlike JWST, which began full operation mere months after launch, ITER won't be fit for purpose for years after its construction ends. The real purpose of ITER—to run high-power fusion experiments using a mixture of the heavy hydrogen isotopes deuterium and tritium—won't happen until more than a decade after the machine hits its first plasma milestone. (Originally those experiments were supposed to take place just five years or so after ITER's debut. Over time, that turned into 10 years: the scheduled 2025 turn-on date would have meant a 2035 start to deuterium-tritium operations.) A further slip to ITER's start date is likely to cause a corresponding delay in the deuterium-tritium experiments.

When assailed by costly, acrimony-inducing delays, the architects of ITER, JWST and other scientific megaprojects typically respond by reminding the public and policymakers that great monuments take time to build. The plans for Notre Dame and other Gothic cathedrals, for example, were of such grand scale and intricacy that, from their outset, everyone knew their creation would span generations; no one present at Notre Dame's beginnings assumed they'd live to see it finished. ITER's designers, however, did not initially hold such lofty expectations for the project. Instead they fully believed they'd see it completed within a couple of decades. Yet the project is now entering its third generation of planning and construction, and its important experiments are at least another generation away. ITER has become the Gothic cathedral of our time: a beautiful but immensely complex structure that we pray will help us find salvation from our energy and climate woes.

Then again, perhaps a cathedral is the wrong metaphor: while Notre Dame took a century to complete, it became an active structure much more quickly, one that was used for its intended purpose less than a generation after construction began. Nobody can say when that will be true for ITER. With each passing decade, this record-breaking monument to big international science looks less and less like a cathedral—and more like a mausoleum.

About the Author

Charles Seife is director of the Arthur L. Carter Institute of Journalism at New York University and the author of seven books, including a history of fusion, Sun in a Bottle, *and a biography of a major scientist,* Hawking Hawking.

Section 3: Can Nuclear Power Fight Climate Change?

How Nuclear Power Can Stop Global Warming

By David Biello

When the *Atlantic Navigator* docked in Baltimore harbor earlier this month, the freighter carried the last remnants of some of the nuclear weapons that the Soviet Union had brandished in the cold war. During the past 20 years more than 19,000 Russian warheads have been dismantled and processed to make fuel for U.S. nuclear reactors. In fact, during that period more than half the uranium fuel that powered the more than 100 reactors in the U.S. came from such reprocessed nuclear weapons.

In addition to reducing the risk of nuclear war, U.S. reactors have also been staving off another global challenge: climate change. The low-carbon electricity produced by such reactors provides 20 percent of the nation's power and, by the estimates of climate scientist James Hansen of Columbia University, avoided 64 billion metric tons of greenhouse gas pollution. They also avoided spewing soot and other air pollution like coal-fired power plants do and thus have saved some 1.8 million lives.

And that's why Hansen, among others, such as former Secretary of Energy Steven Chu, thinks that nuclear power is a key energy technology to fend off catastrophic climate change. "We can't burn all these fossil fuels," Hansen told a group of reporters on December 3, noting that as long as fossil fuels are the cheapest energy source they will continue to be burned. "Coal is almost half the [global] emissions. If you replace these power plants with modern, safe nuclear reactors you could do a lot of [pollution reduction] quickly."

Indeed, he has evidence: the speediest drop in greenhouse gas pollution on record occurred in France in the 1970s and '80s, when that country transitioned from burning fossil fuels to nuclear fission for electricity, lowering its greenhouse emissions by roughly 2 percent per year. The world needs to drop its global warming pollution by 6 percent annually to avoid "dangerous" climate change in the estimation of Hansen and his co-authors in a recent paper in *PLoS One.* "On a global scale, it's hard to see how we could conceivably accomplish this without nuclear," added economist and co-author Jeffrey Sachs, director of the Earth Institute at Columbia University, where Hansen works.

The only problem: the world is not building so many nuclear reactors.

Nuclear Future

China leads the world in new nuclear reactors, with 29 currently under construction and another 59 proposed, according to the World Nuclear Association. And China has not confined itself solely to the typical reactors that employ water and uranium fuel rods; it has built everything from heavy-water reactors originally designed in Canada to a small test fast-reactor.

Yet, even if every planned reactor in China was to be built, the country would still rely on burning coal for more than 50 percent of its electric power–and the Chinese nuclear reactors would provide at best roughly the same amount of energy to the developing nation as does the existing U.S. fleet. Plus, nuclear requires emissions of greenhouse gases for construction, including steel and cement as well as the enrichment of uranium ore required to make nuclear fuel (or the downblending of uranium from nuclear weapons as in the case of the "Megatons to Megawatts" program). Over the full lifetime of a nuclear power plant, that means greenhouse gas emissions of roughly 12 grams of CO_2-equivalent per kilowatt-hour of electricity produced, the same as wind turbines (which also require steel, plastics, rare earths and the like in their construction) and less than photovoltaic panels, according to the U.S. Department of Energy's National Renewable Energy Laboratory.

In other parts of the world nuclear has begun to dwindle. Japan may never restart its nuclear plants in the wake of the multiple meltdowns at Fukushima Daiichi following the earthquake and tsunami in 2011, which also soured public opinion in many parts of the world. Germany still plans to eliminate nuclear power and even France has announced plans to reduce its reliance on reactors. In the U.S. the five new nuclear reactors under construction will replace the four aging reactors that closed in 2013, but as older reactors like Oyster Creek in New Jersey and Vermont Yankee continue to shut down, the number of reactors in the U.S. may be doomed to dwindle as well.

A big problem is cost. The construction of large nuclear power plants requires a lot of money to ensure safety and reliability. For example, for the U.S. to derive one quarter of its total energy supply from nuclear would require building roughly 1,000 new reactors (both to replace old ones and expand the fleet). At today's prices for the two AP-1000 reactors being built in Georgia, such an investment would cost $7 trillion, although that total bill might shrink with an order of that magnitude.

One other idea to cut cost is to begin building smaller reactors of so-called modular design. The Tennessee Valley Authority hopes to catalyze development of such reactors by installing one at its Clinch River site in Tennessee, former home of the U.S.'s failed attempt to build its own commercial fast reactor.

That never-completed breeder reactor is part of a legacy of failed U.S. research and development of new types of reactors, such as the Experimental Breeder Reactor that ran successfully in Idaho for nearly 30 years. "It's a shame that the U.S. essentially stopped R&D on advanced nuclear power a few decades ago," Hansen noted. "By now we should be in a position where a country like China would have some options other than coal."

New Dawn?

That said, nuclear reactors are beginning to get the kind of scientific attention not seen since at least the end of the Cold War. Novel designs with alternative cooling fluids other than water, such as Transatomic Power's molten salt–cooled reactor or the liquid lead–bismuth design from Hyperion Power, are in development. Alternative concepts have attracted funding from billionaires like Bill Gates. Transatomic Power even won the top prize from energy investors at the 2013 summit of the Advanced Research Projects Agency–Energy, or ARPA–E, in 2013. "The intellectual power of what's been done in the nuclear space should allow for radical designs that meet tough requirements," Gates told ARPA–E's 2012 summit, noting that the modeling power of today's supercomputers should allow even more innovation. "When you have fission, you have a million times more energy than when you burn hydrocarbons. That's a nice advantage to have."

ARPA–E itself, however, has no program to develop alternative reactors because of the expense of proving out novel designs and the long timescales required to develop any of them. "We searched a lot in nuclear," ARPA–E's former director Arun Majumdar, now at Google, said in a interview with *Scientific American* earlier this year. "We realized that in the nuclear business, investing $30 [million] to $40 million, I'm not sure it would have moved the needle. ... That is something that I wish I had had the budget to try."

With more money for development of novel designs and public financial support for construction—perhaps as part of a clean energy portfolio standard that lumps in all low-carbon energy sources, not just renewables or a carbon tax—nuclear could be one of the pillars of a three-pronged approach to cutting greenhouse gas emissions: using less energy to do more (or energy efficiency), low-carbon power, and electric cars (as long as they are charged with electricity from clean sources, not coal burning). "The options for large-scale clean electricity are few in number," Sachs noted, including geothermal, hydropower, nuclear, solar and wind. "Each part of the world will have different choices about how to get on a trajectory with most of the energy coming from that list rather than coal."

As long as countries like China or the U.S. employ big grids to deliver electricity, there will be a need for generation from nuclear, coal or gas, the kinds of electricity generation that can be available at all times. A rush to phase out nuclear power privileges natural gas—as is planned under Germany's innovative effort, dubbed the *Energiewende* (energy transition), to increase solar, wind and other renewable power while also eliminating the country's 17 reactors. In fact, Germany hopes to develop technology to store excess electricity from renewable resources as gas to be burned later, a scheme known as "power to gas," according to economist and former German politician Rainer Baake, now director of the energy transition think tank Agora Energiewende. Even worse, a nuclear stall can lead to the construction of more coal-fired power plants, as happened in the U.S. after the end of the nuclear power plant construction era in the 1980s.

Hansen, for one, argues that abundant, clean energy is necessary to lift people out of poverty and begin to reduce greenhouse gas emissions from a swelling human population. Nuclear is one of the technologies available today–and with room for significant improvement and innovation. In that sense, natural gas is a bridge fuel to disaster, even with some form of CO_2 capture and storage, and the world must immediately transition to renewables and nuclear.

But significant hurdles remain, not least the decades required for design, licensing and construction of even existing nuclear technologies, let alone novel ideas. That may mean advanced nuclear power cannot contribute much to efforts to combat climate change in the near term, which leaves current reactor technology as the only short-term nuclear option–and one that is infrequently employed at the global scale at present.

In the same way, U.S. nuclear power plants have not eliminated the threat of nuclear weapons despite 20 years of megatons to megawatts. Russia retains an estimated 8,500 nuclear warheads–and the U.S. some 7,700–despite the best efforts to fission the problem away. The problem of fission and climate change is equally stuck at present. But, as Hansen wrote in an additional assessment of his new analysis, "Environmentalists need to recognize that attempts to force all-renewable policies on all of the world will only assure that fossil fuels continue to reign for base-load electric power, making it unlikely that abundant affordable power will exist and implausible that fossil fuels will be phased out."

About the Author

David Biello is a contributing editor at Scientific American.

We Should Be More Worried about Climate Change Than We Are about Nuclear Power

By Wade Roush

Fifty-four percent of Americans are opponents of nuclear power, according to a 2016 Gallup poll. I can certainly understand why. I used to be one of them. Back in the 1990s, I wrote an entire Ph.D. dissertation about the errors that led to disasters such as Three Mile Island and Chernobyl, and it didn't leave me with much faith in our ability to safely tap fission energy.

But in recent years I've swung around to a different point of view. Today the specter of climate change scares me way more than the risk of future meltdowns. It's time to find ways to enable the nuclear industry's rebirth in the U.S.

The virtue of nuclear plants is that they plug into the existing electrical grid and provide continuous power while emitting zero carbon. Wind and solar are great, too, but we don't yet have the battery technology needed to make them useful as "base-load" power sources.

Without nuclear, it would be much harder to meet the world's growing power needs while limiting the average global temperature increase to 1.5 degrees Celsius, the goal of the 2015 Paris Agreement.

Fortunately, engineers have been rethinking every aspect of reactor design, from the way fuel is packaged to the way cores are cooled. All three active reactors at Japan's Fukushima Daiichi plant melted down in 2011 because an earthquake and the resulting tsunami destroyed the backup diesel generators meant to power cooling pumps. Several companies, including Washington State-based TerraPower, are working on passive designs that would use plain old convection rather than electric pumps to carry away decay heat.

But TerraPower will likely build its first full-scale reactors outside the U.S., vice chairman of the board Nathan Myhrvold told me in a 2017 interview for *Xconomy*. "Frankly, if the whole world was like the United States, we might not have ever done this, because [the U.S. has] gotten so risk-averse that we don't want to try anything new," Myhrvold said.

Today the main obstacle to new nuclear power investment in the U.S. isn't safety, it's cost. Two new Westinghouse Electric Company reactors under construction at Georgia's Vogtle nuclear plant are five years behind schedule and $14 billion over budget.

Builders of traditional reactors have failed to follow basic design, fabrication and supply-chain principles proven in other capital-intensive businesses such as pharmaceuticals and jet engine manufacturing, a 2018 report from the M.I.T. Energy Initiative found.

Then there's the energy marketplace, which was turned upside down by the fracking revolution of the 1990s. In the U.S., natural gas is so cheap and abundant that even well-run nuclear plants can't compete.

They can't, that is, unless one accounts for the social cost of carbon, a measure representing the economic damage that will inevitably result from sea-level rise, wildfires and other consequences of carbon dioxide emissions. If electricity from fossil-fuel plants were taxed to reflect this cost, nuclear would suddenly become the more economical option, the M.I.T. report argues.

Because carbon taxes are a political nonstarter, the states of New York and Illinois are going at it from the other direction, forcing coal- and gas-burning utilities to purchase zero-emissions credits from nuclear plant owners. In both states, courts have turned back power generators' legal challenges to zero-emissions credits, and the new revenue has kept open five plants that faced early closure.

We need to scale up these credits nationally to keep our existing nuclear plants operating while removing obstacles to the construction of safer new designs. If we allow ourselves to be unnerved by the nuclear mistakes of the past, we'll never win the paramount race against global warming.

New Nuclear Power Plants Are Unlikely to Stop the Climate Crisis

By Naomi Oreskes

Last fall my Harvard University class and I went through an exercise to help the students understand how the world might address the climate crisis and keep the average global temperature increase below two degrees Celsius. Guided by John Sterman, a management professor at the Massachusetts Institute of Technology, the students pretended to be climate negotiators, offering or blocking climate policies. Then, using En-ROADS, a computer simulation of the effects of climate policies that Sterman co-developed, they were able to see the consequences of their proposals on the 2100 average global temperature.

The exercise offered both bad news and good. The bad news is that keeping the rise in temperature below 2° C is going to be very hard and holding it under 1.5° probably impossible. The good news is that the challenge can be met–if we implement a large portfolio of solutions, the most important of which are eliminating fossil-fuel subsidies and putting a stiff price on carbon.

None of this will come as a shock to climate experts: our results were consistent with numerous reports that have argued against the silver bullet approach and in favor of "silver buckshot." But several things surprised the students. One was that planting a trillion trees doesn't help much, because it takes too long for them to grow. Another was that nuclear power doesn't help either, for essentially the same reason: nuclear plants take too long to build and bring online. Globally, the average construction time is about 10 years, and you need to add many years on to that period for site selection, regulatory approval and licensing. Some notorious examples have taken much longer. The most recent nuclear power reactors built in the U.S., at Georgia Power's Vogtle plant, were started in 2013 and are still not finished. That's the problem with imagined "breakthrough" technologies, too. Breakthroughs can be sudden, but implementation is slow.

I left the class thinking about nuclear power. Many people think nuclear energy is going to be the climate solution (or at least a big part of it). President Barack Obama included federal loan guarantees for nuclear power in his energy plan, in the hopes of jump-starting construction and garnering Republican support. (It did neither, but some Republicans are now pushing nuclear power as the key to cleaner U.S. energy.) If I want to rile up my Twitter feed, all I need do is post something even faintly skeptical about nuclear power, and its advocates come out in force, accusing me of being a Luddite, or a troglodyte, or worse.

What is it about nuclear energy that makes its advocates so determined in the face of what should be discouraging facts? After all, unlike futuristic, untried technologies, we have plenty of facts about this one, and most of them are discouraging.

The first American civilian nuclear power plant broke ground in Pennsylvania in 1954, around the same time that physicist John von Neumann predicted that, within a few decades, nuclear power would be so efficient as to make energy "free –just like the unmetered air–with coal and oil used mainly as raw materials for organic chemical synthesis." That didn't happen. Today nuclear power remains the most expensive form of electricity generation in the U.S.–typically costing twice as much to operate as a fossil-fuel-based plant. While the price of renewables has dropped dramatically, the cost of nuclear has remained stubbornly high. Nuclear fission is a technology with a track record of overpromising and underdelivering.

Why then do so many people keep coming back to it? I've come to think it's the same reason people turn to geoengineering and nuclear fusion (which has been "just around the corner" since 1943): the promise of technological progress. For the past century or more, humans have been accustomed to technological breakthroughs that made life easier, more comfortable and more entertaining. But climate change throws future advancement into doubt. It breaks the promise of progress. No matter what we do, we are going to be paying for the costs of our historical and current use of fossil fuels for decades to come.

So we turn to technofideism—the faith that technology will save us. Perhaps it will. But perhaps it won't, and our long-standing patterns of behavior will have to change along with our technology. And that's a hard pill to swallow.

About the Author

Naomi Oreskes is a professor of the history of science at Harvard University. She is author of Why Trust Science? *(Princeton University Press, 2019) and co-author of* The Big Myth *(Bloomsbury, 2023).*

Section 4: Safety Concerns

What Happens During a Nuclear Meltdown?

By John Matson

Nuclear reactors at the Fukushima Daiichi station in Japan are critically endangered but have not reached full meltdown status. Our nuclear primer explains what that means and how the situation compares with past nuclear accidents.

Q: How does a nuclear reactor work?

A: Most nuclear reactors, including those at Japan's Fukushima Daiichi generating station, are essentially high-tech kettles that efficiently boil water to produce electricity. They rely on harnessing nuclear fission–the splitting of an atom into two smaller atoms, which also yields heat and sends neutrons flying. If another atom absorbs one of those neutrons, the atom becomes unstable and undergoes fission itself, releasing more heat and more neutrons. The chain reaction becomes self-sustaining, producing a steady supply of heat to boil water, drive steam turbines and thereby generate electricity.

Q: How much electricity does nuclear power provide in Japan and elsewhere?

A: With 54 nuclear reactors generating 280 billion kilowatt-hours annually, Japan is the world's third-largest producer of nuclear power, after the U.S. and France, according to data from the International Atomic Energy Agency. The Fukushima Daiichi station, which has been hit hard by the March 11 earthquake, houses six of those reactors, all of which came online in the 1970s.

Worldwide, nuclear energy accounts for about 15 percent of electricity generation; Japan gets nearly 30 percent of its electricity from its nuclear plants. The U.S. produces more nuclear power overall, but nuclear constitutes a smaller share of its energy portfolio. About 20 percent of U.S. electricity comes from nuclear power plants, making it the third-largest source of electricity in the country after coal (45 percent) and natural gas (23 percent).

Q: What fuels a nuclear reactor?

A: Most nuclear reactors use uranium fuel that has been "enriched" in uranium 235, an isotope of uranium that fissions readily. (Isotopes are variants of elements with different atomic masses.) Uranium 238 is much more common in nature than uranium 235 but does not fission well, so fuel manufacturers boost the uranium 235 content to a few percent, which is enough to maintain a continuous fission reaction and generate electricity. Enriched uranium is manufactured into fuel rods that are encased in metal cladding made of alloys such as zirconium.

Reactor No. 3 at the Fukushima Daiichi station runs on so-called mixed oxide (MOX) fuel, in which uranium is mixed with other fissile materials such as plutonium from spent reactor fuel or from decommissioned nuclear weapons.

Q: How do you turn off a nuclear reaction?

A: Sustained nuclear fission reactions rely on the passing of neutrons from one atom to another–the neutrons released in one atom's fissioning trigger the fissioning of the next atom. The way to cut off a fission chain reaction, then, is to intercept the neutrons. Nuclear reactors utilize control rods made from elements such as cadmium, boron or hafnium, all of which are efficient neutron absorbers. When the reactor malfunctions or when operators need to shut off the reactor for any other reason, technicians can remotely plunge control rods into the reactor core to soak up neutrons and shut down the nuclear reaction.

Q: Can a reactor melt down once the nuclear reaction is stopped?

A: Even after the control rods have done their job and arrested the fission reaction, the fuel rods retain a great deal of heat. What is more, the uranium atoms that have already split in two produce radioactive by-products that themselves give off a great deal of heat. So the reactor core continues to produce heat in the absence of fissioning.

If the rest of the reactor is operating normally, pumps will continue to circulate coolant (usually water) to carry away the reactor core's heat. In Japan the March 11 earthquake and tsunami caused blackouts that cut off the externally sourced AC power for the reactors' cooling system. According to published reports, backup diesel generators at the power plant failed shortly thereafter, leaving the reactors uncooled and in serious danger of overheating.

Without a steady coolant supply, a hot reactor core will continuously boil off the water surrounding it until the fuel is no longer immersed. If fuel rods remain uncovered, they may begin to melt, and hot, radioactive fuel can pool at the bottom of the vessel containing the reactor. In a worst-case meltdown scenario the puddle of hot fuel could melt through the steel containment vessel and through subsequent barriers meant to contain the nuclear material, exposing massive quantities of radioactivity to the outside world.

Q: How can a meltdown be averted?

A: The Japanese plant's operators have made a number of attempts to cool the reactors, including pumping seawater into the reactor core to replenish the dwindling cooling fluid. The Tokyo Electric Power Company has also injected boric acid, an absorber of neutrons, into the reactors.

Q: How does this incident compare with Chernobyl or Three Mile Island?

A: At present, three of the reactors at Fukushima Daiichi station are seriously crippled. Units 1 and 3 have experienced explosions that destroyed exterior walls, apparently from buildups of hydrogen gas produced by the zirconium in the fuel rods reacting with coolant water at extremely high temperatures–but the interior containment vessels there thus far seem to be intact. A third explosion was reported March 15 at reactor No. 2, and the situation there appears direr. Pressure in the suppression pool—a doughnut-shaped water vessel below the reactor—dropped after the explosion, indicating that the containment vessel had been compromised.

In reactor Nos. 1, 2 and 3 water levels dropped enough to leave the fuel assemblies temporarily uncovered; those fuel rods are presumed to have suffered damage. And a fire at a pool storing spent fuel rods at dormant reactor No. 4 is posing additional hazards to the few workers remaining at the site.

Japanese officials initially rated the incident a level 4, an "accident with local consequences," on the seven-tier International Nuclear and Radiological Event Scale (INES), but Princeton University physicist Frank von Hippel told *The New York Times* that the Fukushima Daiichi situation is "way past Three Mile Island already." Three Mile Island, the highest-profile U.S. nuclear accident, was classified level 5—an "accident with wider consequences".

At that Pennsylvania nuclear station in 1979 a cooling malfunction combined with worker error led to a partial meltdown—about half of the reactor core melted and formed a radioactive puddle at the bottom of the steel pressure vessel. The vessel remained intact, but some radiation did escape from the plant into the surrounding environment.

The 1986 Chernobyl accident was far more devastating; it rates as a 7, or a "major accident," on the INES scale. In Ukraine, then part of the Soviet Union, a power surge caused an explosion in one of the plant's reactors, releasing huge doses of radioactive fallout into the air. Two plant workers died within hours, according to the U.S. Nuclear Regulatory Commission; 28 more died in the following months from radiation poisoning. The fallout from Chernobyl was widespread, and the health effects of the disaster are difficult to quantify. A report from the United Nations Scientific Committee on the Effects of Atomic Radiation found that 6,000 individuals who were under the age of 18 in Ukraine, Belarus or Russia at the time of the disaster had by 2006 contracted thyroid cancer, "a substantial fraction" of whom likely contracted the disease due to radiation exposure.

About the Author

John Matson is a former reporter and editor for Scientific American *who has written extensively about astronomy and physics.*

Deconstructing John Miller's Arguments Against Nuclear Energy in the *New York Times*

By Ashutosh Jogalekar

John Miller, a social psychologist and journalist who once served as an officer on a nuclear submarine has a piece on Andrew Revkin's *New York Times* blog *Dot Earth* in which he purportedly dismisses several claims about nuclear energy and provides evidence to the contrary; these include general claims as well as those made more specifically in the film "Pandora's Promise" which I reviewed on this blog earlier. Since I found much of merit in the film, it's obvious that I disagree with most of Miller's points. Based on his replies to comments, Miller seems to think that providing a lot of links is tantamount to providing evidence. But this is a flawed assumption; for instance I might write a piece on alien abductions that is rife with links, and yet my arguments may not make much sense. What is strange in Miller's piece though is that several of the links which he provides to support his arguments *themselves* contain information either contradicting or qualifying his claims. Below we look at a few of his arguments.

Miller cites a WHO study and claims that Chernobyl killed 16,000 people. However if we follow his link we find the following important qualifier which is noted right below the numerical estimate:

> *While these figures all reflect human suffering and death, they nevertheless represent only a very small fraction of the total number of cancers seen since the accident and expected in the future in Europe. Indeed, our analysis of the trends in cancer incidence and mortality does not demonstrate any increase that can be clearly attributed to the Chernobyl accident. The exception is thyroid cancer, which, over ten years ago, was already shown to be increased in the most contaminated regions around the site of the accident.*

It's worth noting that this qualification is common to all estimates of cancers from accidents like Chernobyl; the number is small to begin with, but even higher numbers are a fraction of the number of natural cancers that would occur over the years. Thus it is very difficult to ascribe any particular cancer to a radiation accident. Plus, thyroid cancer is easily curable and in the case of Chernobyl resulted from the failure of a highly bureaucratic and secretive Communist system to sound the alarm, take prompt action and distribute iodine pills, a situation unlikely to arise in other cases. It's worth constantly reminding ourselves that Chernobyl represents a close to worst-case scenario resulting from a fundamentally flawed design that has happened exactly once. Citing Chernobyl as a strike against nuclear would be like citing Bhopal (which definitively killed many more than Chernobyl) as a strike against the chemical industry.

Miller also says that fast reactors utilizing sodium are unsafe. To support his claims he links to a 1956 study by Nobel Laureate Hans Bethe that calculates the explosive yield of a fast sodium-cooled reactor should all the coolant suddenly disappear. Miller's argument here is extremely limited and misleading. Let's start by noting that throughout his life, Hans Bethe was a champion of nuclear power, for instance penning a clear-headed essay in 1976 on the need for nuclear power in the pages of this very publication. But let's take a look at the study; for one thing, Bethe's calculation assumes a worst-case scenario:

"A number of pessimistically simplifying assumptions are made, in particular the rate of increase of reactivity is calculated assuming that the core suddenly loses its cohesion and collapses under the gravity."

Such a worst-case scenario cannot be cited as the norm. In addition, in spite of minor leaks and problems, there has been no major accident with a fast reactor even close to that envisioned by Bethe that causes a loss of life. In fact fast breeder reactor construction continues in many countries. Neither are fast breeder reactors the only game in the nuclear town.

Finally, it is pure scaremongering to say that the reactor can become a "small unintended atom bomb" even in the worst case scenario. In the 1956 study Bethe calculates the energy release from even a catastrophic accident as equivalent to *160 kg* of TNT. This is a large explosion, but not even remotely close to an atomic bomb; for comparison, the bomb dropped on Hiroshima–quite small by modern standards–released about *16,000 tons* of TNT. Even one of the smallest known nuclear weapons, the Davy Crockett tactical nuke, released 10 to 20 tons of TNT. It is also a well known fact that fundamental physics prevents a nuclear reactor from exploding like an atomic bomb (also, what does the random link to a book on Fast Spectrum Reactors mean?).

Miller's statements about plutonium are also misleading and incomplete. He cites plutonium as causing lung cancers, but plutonium can cause harm only when inhaled; there are poisons like botulism toxin and anthrax spores which are far more easily available and much more dangerous. Plutonium is one of those things that needs to be deposited in a very precise location to cause harm; by that token, in one expert's words, "tomorrow's production of hatpins could kill everyone if placed in their lungs." In addition plutonium is not something that you can buy off the shelf. Saying "Procure 29 pounds [of] plutonium and you can build a bomb with it" completely ignores the security measures taken to safeguard the substance and the extreme difficulty that anyone trying to obtain even a gram of it will face. Personally I would be much more scared of the guy who can procure 29 pounds of cheap and easily available nitrate fertilizer.

Later Miller decides to criticize some of the people interviewed in the film "Pandora's Promise" and their apparently misleading statements. In the process Miller says a lot of misleading and incomplete things himself. For instance he points to a NREL study that examines various scenarios for achieving a 80% dependence on renewables by 2050, but does not point to the simplifying assumptions that the study makes and the huge political and economic challenges it considers; that does not mean research in renewables is futile, but it certainly makes a good case at the very least for an equal push in nuclear research. Miller also cites a 2009 McKinsey study that calculates a possible 23% cut in non-transporation energy use, but he does not cite the $520 billion price tag. The point is this: if we are willing to spend so much on unproven renewables based on so many simplifying assumptions, there is really no good case against spending about as much on modifying existing nuclear power plants and exploring new designs.

Miller also makes the non-statement that "Standing near a nuclear spent fuel rod will kill you" and uses this as an argument against reactors. Why on earth would anyone stand near a spent fuel rod? That would be like arguing that drinking a gallon of gasoline would kill you and that this is a good argument against using gasoline in cars.

Later Miller takes environmentalist Gwyneth Cravens to task. In the film, Cravens says that drinking tritium-lade water for a day would release no more radiation in your body than eating a banana. He links to a piece by Ed Lyman challenging this comparison, but a quick look at the comments section indicates arguments (most notably by Rod Adams) that significantly temper Lyman's calculation. In addition Miller misses Cravens's more general argument: that nuclear reactors release a lot of artificial radioactivity at doses that are much smaller than natural radiation levels. A short while later Miller sets up another straw man and says that if Fukushima had AP1000 reactors they would have withstood a loss of power for only 3 days. Firstly, the AP1000 is not the only game in town. Secondly, Fukushima was in the unfortunate situation of being hit by a double whammy; a massive earthquake followed by a massive tsunami. By any definition this is a rare event unlikely to happen in stable geological sites located inland. In addition the tsunami and earthquake killed tens of thousands, while according to the most recent WHO report, the nuclear accident will likely cause no excess fatal cancers.

Generally speaking then, I found Miller's piece to be largely misleading and alarmist, indulging in much cherry-picking, citing worst-case scenarios and and linking to pieces which he himself must have known to be much more measured and critical of the arguments that he makes. His piece is also quite incomplete; for instance there is no mention of nuclear energy successes like France or of entrepreneurs like Bill Gates funding promising new reactor designs. There's more to nuclear energy than what Miller would have us believe.

This article was published in Scientific American's *former blog network and reflects the views of the author, not necessarily those of* Scientific American.

About the Author

Ashutosh Jogalekar is a chemist interested in the history, philosophy and sociology of science. He is fascinated by the logic of scientific discovery and by the interaction of science with public sentiments and policy. He blogs at The Curious Wavefunction and can be reached at curiouswavefunction@gmail.com.

Chernobyl Didn't Kill Nuclear Power

By Frank N. von Hippel

Thirty years ago, at 1:24 A.M. on April 26, 1986, explosions blew the lid and roof off the Chernobyl Unit 4 nuclear reactor in Ukraine, in the former Soviet Union, blasting radioactive material into the atmosphere. The outflow, driven by a raging fire within the reactor core, blew in all directions during the following week. Ultimately an area of 3,110 square kilometers was contaminated with cesium 137, to a level requiring evacuation.

Superficially, it is reasonable to leap to the conclusion that fear generated by the Chernobyl disaster turned the public against nuclear power—so strongly that even now, three decades later, there is serious doubt that it will ever be a major alternative to climate-threatening fossil fuels. In the 15 years before the Chernobyl accident, an average of about 20 new nuclear power reactors came online each year. Five years after the accident, the average had dropped to four a year.

But the full story is more complex. The effects of Chernobyl on people, though significant, were not devastating. Beyond the evacuation area, it is estimated that the radiation will cause tens of thousands cases of cancer across Europe over 80 years. That may sound like a large number, but it is a mostly undetectable addition to the background cancer rate. One exception is thyroid cancer, caused by the ingestion of radioactive iodides: there have been visible epidemics—only 1 to 2 percent fatal, fortunately—in the most affected regions of Belarus, Russia and Ukraine.

Despite the projected cancer deaths from Chernobyl and the 2011 Fukushima Daiichi disaster in Japan, however, nuclear power still appears safer than coal, measured in terms of average deaths per unit of electric energy generated. According to a 2010 study by the National Research Council, if the U.S.'s then 104 nuclear reactors had been replaced in 2005 with coal plants, the increased air pollution would have caused thousands of additional premature deaths annually.

People also tend to worry more, however, about the long-term impact of radiation than they do about the effects of air pollution. A survey of the psychological well-being of Ukraine's population 20 years after Chernobyl found that an extra radiation dose equivalent to one year's natural background exposure was correlated with reduced life satisfaction, an increase in diagnosed mental disorders and a reduction in subjective life expectancy.

Such worries contributed to the drop in new plant construction post-Chernobyl, but there were other reasons. One was that the growth of electric power consumption in developed countries slowed dramatically at around the same time because the price of electricity stopped falling. In 1974 the U.S. Atomic Energy Commission was projecting that the U.S. would require the equivalent of 3,000 large nuclear power reactors by 2016. Today it would take just 500 such plants to generate as much electricity as we consume on average–although more capacity would be required for times of peak consumption.

Another factor is that, contrary to the claims of boosters in the 1950s that nuclear power would be "too cheap to meter," it is quite expensive. Fuel costs are low, but construction costs are huge, especially in North America and Europe–$6 billion to $12 billion per reactor. This expense has been driven in part by more stringent safety standards but also by the fact that, with fewer plants being built, there are fewer construction workers qualified to build them, resulting in costly construction delays for corrections of mistakes. The future of nuclear power is now largely in the hands of China. About half of the nuclear power reactors under construction starting in 2008 are located there, and China's nuclear industry is beginning to propose projects in other countries. China's rate of construction is still far below that of the U.S. and Western Europe in the 1970s, however, and the world is consuming electric power at three times the rate it did then. The International Energy Agency projects that the nuclear share of China's electricity generation will grow to only 10 percent by 2040.

On the scale needed to shift human energy use away from fossil fuels, therefore, nuclear power has become a helpful but relatively marginal player. Chernobyl damaged its prospects, but it was not the only reason for the technology's decline.

About the Author

Frank N. von Hippel is a senior research physicist and professor of public and international affairs emeritus with Princeton's Program on Science and Global Security. He is a member of the Steering Committee of the Physicists Coalition for Nuclear Threat Reduction.

The Risks of Russian Attacks near Ukraine's Nuclear Power Plants

By Andrea Thompson; edited by Dean Visser

Editor's Note (8/15/22): Recent shelling around the Zaporizhzhia nuclear power plant in Ukraine is renewing concerns about damage to the plant initially raised when Russian forces first attacked the facility in March.

People around the world watched via livestreamed security camera as Russian forces attacked and took over Ukraine's Zaporizhzhia nuclear power plant—the largest in Europe—on Friday morning local time. Amid the shelling and gunfire, a fire broke out at a training facility in the complex and was later extinguished, according to news reports. The incident raised alarm among world leaders and nuclear experts about the potential for purposeful or accidental reactor damage that could cause radiation leaks or, in a worst-case scenario, reactor core meltdowns.

Rafael Grossi, director general of the International Atomic Energy Agency (IAEA), told the United Nations Security Council that the plant's operations were normal after the attack and has said that no radioactive material was released. But he and other nuclear experts have warned that there is a danger of accidents there and at other nuclear plants in Ukraine as the conflict continues.

Scientific American spoke with Edwin Lyman, director of nuclear power safety at the Union of Concerned Scientists, to explain the concerns about such facilities during wartime and to talk about some of the safety measures that are in place.

[An edited transcript of the interview follows.]

Q: What type of reactors does the Zaporizhzhia complex have, and how might they differ from those at Chernobyl or U.S. nuclear power plants?

A: The six reactors at Zaporizhzhia are called VVER-1000s, and they are cooled and moderated by light [ordinary] water. So in that respect, they're similar to U.S. pressurized water reactors. They are somewhat more advanced models than the earlier versions of [this type of reactor], so they do have some features that are more in line with modern safety philosophy—but not entirely. And they're different from the Chernobyl-type reactors, called RBMKs, which used a different moderator material—graphite—and had a lot of technical flaws, which contributed to the occurrence and the severity of the [Chernobyl] accident in 1986. So the type of accident that occurred at Chernobyl, which is essentially a power excursion, is very unlikely in a light water reactor.

In any nuclear reactor, the purpose is to maintain a nuclear fission chain reaction in the fuel that generates heat and also additional neutrons, which are used to propagate the chain reaction. When uranium atoms fission, they release heat, so the fuel gets hot. Water in this type of reactor is pumped through the core and is heated and then is transferred to another loop that's under high pressure. And then it's transferred to another system of steam generators, where water is turned into steam, and that turns a turbine.

These [Zaporizhzhia reactors] were designed in the Soviet Union, and they date as far back as the early 1980s. So they are past their expiration date, but the Ukrainians extended their licenses.

Q: Does the age of the reactors factor into the safety concerns here?

A: Well, it always has to be taken into account, because they got license extensions. They have been refurbished to some extent, but there are always systems that can't be replaced. For instance, the vessel that holds the reactor fuel—and which becomes embrittled over time—that poses a risk in certain types of accidents, so you do have to factor it in.

Q: What are the kinds of safety systems that this type of reactor would have against accidents?

A: The big danger in any nuclear reactor is that somehow cooling of the fuel is disrupted, because without enough cooling, the fuel will heat up to the point where it can destroy itself. This is what happened, to a lesser extent, at Three Mile Island [in Pennsylvania in 1979] and, to a greater extent, at Fukushima [in Japan] in 2011. In addition, these plants store their spent nuclear fuel on-site–and some of that fuel is stored in cooling water, which also has to be replenished with pumps.

The modern reactors of this type have emergency core cooling systems so that, if there's a breach in a cooling pipe, they have systems that can inject emergency coolant directly. And these [VVER-1000s] do have those kinds of systems, unlike some of the earlier versions of these Soviet reactors.

In addition to a pipe break, you can have a loss of power, which is what affected Fukushima. These plants normally draw electricity from the grid to operate their systems, and if that's interrupted, they have to rely on backup power with emergency diesel generators. Each reactor has three, and then there are a couple extra, so there are a lot a lot of backup diesels at the plant. But there's always the possibility that something happens that can disable multiple units at once–like at Fukushima, where the site was flooded, and even though they had plenty of backup diesels, they stopped operating. After Fukushima, as in many other countries, Ukraine developed additional measures to cope with that kind of Fukushima-like accident, where there's a long-duration loss of electrical power. And that included acquiring additional mobile pumps that do not require electricity and run on diesel fuel.

Q: What are the main concerns with fighting at or near these nuclear facilities?

A: Clearly there's the potential for many different kinds of damage: either direct, destructive damage to the plant systems, safety systems, infrastructure or indirect damage to support systems such as the off-site power. And [there is] potential for fire, which can propagate and disable the instrumentation control system. Very few of those are addressed that would need to be, if you're going to worry that there is a real possibility of having this plant in the middle of a war zone.

I guess the moral is that if you want to potentially seriously damage the plant, you don't have to go after the containment building, which is the hardest part. There are other systems that are not as well protected. But even those containment buildings are not necessarily able to withstand certain types of military attack. Even if they are not breached, they can spall, and you can have concrete falling down onto the reactor vessel. Or just strong vibrations might also cause damage.

Q: Before this attack, was there growing concern in the nuclear community that something like this could happen and potentially cause accidents?

A: It's sort of like an unspoken fear. There have been certain individuals who have raised this for a long time, but these concerns have basically been dismissed. There are a lot of concerns you can have about nuclear power, and some of them seem very improbable–and until they happen, people tend to dismiss them. And this is one example.

The cost of hardening commercial nuclear power plants so that they might survive a military onslaught is probably prohibitive. At the beginning of the nuclear era, people such as Edward Teller [a theoretical physicist and member of the Manhattan Project] thought nuclear power plants needed to be underground.

Q: If there were damage at the Zaporizhzhia plant, what kind of explosion or radiation leakage might happen?

A: It depends on the progression of the accident, how severe it is and whether these emergency measures can be brought to bear or not. In the worst case, if you have an unmitigated loss of cooling capability, the nuclear fuel can overheat and melt and burn through the steel reactor vessel that holds it and drop to the floor of the container. And in that case, the containment is the only remaining barrier between the radioactive material in the reactor and the environment. It's designed to withstand certain types of events but not others.

At Three Mile Island, the core partially melted, but operators were able to stop in time—before it reached the point where it melted through the reactor vessel. But even then, from the fuel that was damaged, there were a lot of radioactive gases that were generated and had to be vented, though they had relatively low radiotoxicity. If the containment is not breached, they do leak—no building can be perfectly tight. But that leakage is designed and tested to be relatively low. [In] the U.S., there's a regulatory limit for how bad an accident can get in terms of exposure to the public, and the safety systems and the containment have been designed to meet that. But, again, that assumes certain things about what the nature of the accident is that can prove to be false or can be exceeded, such as at Fukushima.

I think the particular type of release from Chernobyl—which was pretty large and was injected high into the atmosphere and was widely distributed—that's probably less likely with a reactor like this. If you look at Fukushima, the releases were smaller, and they didn't disperse over as wide an area. It's certainly a regional concern. But if multiple reactors are affected at the same time, if the spent fuel is damaged, if the containment is mechanically breached, then all bets are off.

Q: Reports indicate that after the Russian takeover of the Chernobyl site in Ukraine, its staff are still working and have been unable to switch out. What are the concerns there and at Zaporizhzhia if shifts are unable to relieve one another?

A: Well, having well-rested operators is critical because the tasks they have to perform are complex, and they need to be alert. You have to ensure that fatigue is being monitored. If there's a plant staff, and they're not getting any relief, and they can't go home, and they're working under duress, it's a dangerous combination. There will have to be measures for that.

Q: What do combatants and the IAEA need to do?

A: The IAEA doesn't have very much authority in this area, and I see the director general, Grossi, is struggling with this. He made this offer to go to Chernobyl and negotiate some sort of deal. But it's not clear exactly what, and it's going to depend on the good graces of the parties. That means addressing this in the context of a military conflict.

Ukraine and Russia have agreed on these temporary ceasefires in particular zones for safe passage of the population, and they could model that until they've reached some sort of an agreement on how nuclear power plants are going to be operated.

This raises these difficult issues of how far Ukraine would go to prevent a military takeover of a nuclear power plant and the potential for damage.

About the Author

Andrea Thompson is an associate editor covering the environment, energy and earth sciences. She has been covering these issues for 16 years. Prior to joining Scientific American, *she was a senior writer covering climate science at Climate Central and a reporter and editor at Live Science, where she primarily covered earth science and the environment. She has moderated panels, including as part of the United Nations Sustainable Development Media Zone, and appeared in radio and television interviews on major networks. She holds a graduate degree in science, health and environmental reporting from New York University, as well as a B.S. and an M.S. in atmospheric chemistry from the Georgia Institute of Technology. Follow Thompson on Bluesky @andreatweather.bsky.social*

Section 5: Handling Nuclear Waste

A (Radioactive) Cut in the Earth That Will Not Stay Closed

By Tom Zoellner

Editor's Note: The following is an excerpt from Tom Zoellner's book *Uranium*.

One of the most potentially dangerous places in the world is called *Shinkolobwe*, the name of a now-destroyed village in central Africa which took its name from a thorny fruit resembling an apple. After boiling, the outside of the fruit cools quickly but the inside is like a sponge. It retains hot water for a long time. Squeezing it results in a burn.

The word is also local slang for a man who is easygoing on the surface but becomes angry when provoked.

A local story around Shinkolobwe says that a deep pit near the remnants of the village is haunted by a spirit named "Madame Kipese," who lives inside the pit. The Madame had been a lively and forceful woman when she was alive, but had grown evil after her death and burial. White men had come here many years ago to dig the hole and had become friendly with her. They may have even had sex with her.

Madame Kipese needs to consume human souls to keep herself strong. She emerges from time to time to kill someone. Unexplained deaths in the area are sometimes attributed to Madame Kipese.

"I would not go there myself," an officer from the federal police told me. He was on the protection staff of Joseph Kabila, the president of the Democratic Republic of the Congo.

"It's a very dangerous place," he went on. "Cell phones burn out when you take them there. Television sets won't work, even if there were a place to plug them in. Be sure you don't wear a T-shirt. You must wear a long-sleeve shirt to protect yourself from the dust. All the men who work there are supposed to wear long-sleeve shirts.

Try not to breathe the dust. Whatever you do, don't put any of that stuff in your pocket.

"Are you sure you want to go?"

I told him I was sure.

"You have to cross through at least four roadblocks before you get there," he said. "Each one is more serious. That place is very heavily guarded. It is considered a strategic site. They want to make sure you are not a saboteur. The last line of defense is a squad of United Nations soldiers. I won't be able to help you with them."

I wound up paying him $80 for what he described as a special police authorization.

The next day, I received a photocopy with the Presidential letterhead upon it. Below it, in blue ballpoint scrawl, was my name, my passport number, my birthday and a series of villages I was to pass through on my way.

Shinkolobwe is now considered an official nonplace. The provincial governor had ordered a squad of soldiers to evacuate the village and burn down all the huts in 2004, leaving nothing behind but stumps and garbage. A detachment of Army personnel was left behind to guard the edges and make sure nobody entered.

The government had been embarrassed by a series of accidental deaths inside the mine. Some men were digging inside a jerry-built tunnel when it collapsed on them. Eight were killed, and thirteen injured.

Fatal accidents are all too common in the illegal mining trade of the Congo. Abandoned mines like this one are scattered all over the southern savanna and most of them are still being picked over by local farmers hoping to boost their income by selling a few bags of minerals on the side, usually copper and a smattering of cobalt. Shinkolobwe was different. This was the pit which, in the 1940s, had yielded most of the uranium for the atomic bombs the United States had dropped on Hiroshima and Nagasaki.

But it was more than historical curiosity. The pit had been closed and the mineshafts sealed tight with concrete plugs when Congo became an independent nation more than four decades ago, yet local miners had been sneaking into the pit to dig out its radioactive contents and sell them on the black market. The birthplace of the atomic bomb is still bleeding uranium and nobody is certain where it might be going.

Shinkolobwe is in the midst of a pleasant savanna of hills and acacia trees in a region called Katanga, where people have been farming more than two thousand years with tools made from wood and copper picked from the ground. This place, and the rest of the Congo, had been the private preserve of King Leopold II of Belgium, who had claimed the territory for himself when the European powers were beginning to plant their flags around Africa in the 1870s. Leopold promised to run "this magnificent African cake" for the charity and benefit of the natives.

Congo instead became a gigantic forced-labor camp. The Africans were threatened with brutal beatings and the amputation of their hands and even beheadings if they failed to collect enough ivory tusks or lumber to satisfy the quotas of Belgian managers. The government of Belgium took over the estates in 1908, preserving the system of forced labor under the rule of monopoly companies. The largest was a mining giant called "Union Minière de Haut Katanga" which started exploiting copper in the southern tail section. Delighted executives called it *un scandale géologique*–a "geological scandal"–and built an empire of mills, furnaces and rails in the bush. Locals were paid the equivalent of twenty cents a day to break rocks and push carts. It amounted to a version of debt slavery: taxes were kept purposefully high and workers were not permitted to select their own occupations. The men slept eight to a hut in settlements ringed with barbed wire to prevent them from leaving before their contracts were up. Typhoid and dysentery were rampant.

One of these sites had been Shinkolobwe, where patches of high-grade uranium had been found by chance in 1915. The workers were made to carry sacks of the velvety black stone–then used only for radium-based cancer cures–more than twenty kilometers to the railhead, where they were sent to port and then shipped by ocean steamer to Belgium. The tailings were simply thrown away. By itself, it was considered worthless: a trash rock.

When the Nazis invaded Belgium in 1940, the company moved its headquarters to New York. The U.S. would soon become the world's largest user of its cobalt, which was an important metal for the manufacture of aircraft engines. The Congo mines started operating around the clock. And by then, an ominous realization had began to dawn among a handful of scientists in European and American universities: that the overburdened nucleus of U-235 was just on the edge of cracking asunder and might be broken with a single neutron. The mine would go on to supply nearly two-thirds of the uranium used in the bomb dropped over Hiroshima, and much of the related product of plutonium that went into the bomb dropped on Nagasaki.

For the next two decades, Shinkolobwe enjoyed a mystique as the number-one producer of the most powerful substance on earth. "A freak occurrence in nature," one Army colonel called it. "Nothing like it has ever again been found." Access to the site was forbidden, and the closest a visitor could get was to see the giant block of pure uranium the company put on display in the nearby city of Elisabethville. Visitors were warned not to get too close with their cameras, lest their film be fogged and ruined. A sign said: *Attention. Bloc Radioactif*!

The Belgians had expected to rule their colony for more than a century, but increasing violence in the capital convinced them to step aside and grant Congo its independence in 1960. With American backing, a 29-year-old army officer named Joseph Desiree Mobutu seized power in a coup and would, over time, set himself up as a secular messiah even as he looted the nation as systematically as King Leopold. He took a cut from virtually every business in his country, siphoning off $4 billion, and building luxurious marble palaces for himself all over his dirt-poor country. The once-promising economy went into a tailspin. Roads fell apart. Farms dehydrated in the equatorial sun. Union Minière's property was nationalized, and then looted.

But not Shinkolobwe. The managers feared that such a lethal substance would fall into the wrong hands. They poured concrete into the shafts and carted off the equipment. Scavengers tore the metal from the uranium warehouses. The worker's village was evacuated and sealed off, and weeds began to sprout inside the shells of brick townhouses. Mango trees drooped, nodded and eventually toppled onto the deserted streets. Shinkolobwe crept back, day after day, into a state of nature.

The place does not appear on most local maps, but is not difficult to find. I hired a translator and we rented a Toyota Land Cruiser for a few hundred dollars in the city of Lubumbashi, once called Elisabethville, the principal railhead for most of the ore trains that used to run to the Atlantic. The city's economy still thrives on minerals, both legal and bootleg. Chinese companies have established a strong presence as buyers of the copper and cobalt picked out of the open pits.

We left the city at dawn and headed north, on a potholed national highway that faded into dirt, through forests of eucalyptus and acacia. My translator turned onto a rutted side track in the hilly country north of Likasi and we quickly got bogged down in the mud. A farmer came to help push us out; a man named Alphonse Ngoy Somwe, who told us that he had worked as a miner at Shinkolobwe, where copper was usually the big thing. There had been at least one time, however, when he had looked for uranium. A few years ago, he recalled, some white men had come to buy their ore and had waved electronic devices over the rocks. He said he didn't want to do mining anymore–"it kills"–but after we pushed the Toyota loose, he agreed to show us the way.

We bounced through a small village with a Pentecostal church made out of poles and grass and, shortly thereafter, came to a spot where the road took a plunge into a rocky valley; too precipitous for the Land Cruiser to handle.

Sowme told us the mine was about seven kilometers further. I shouldered my pack and we all started walking.

A substantial amount of uranium has been smuggled out of Congo in the last decade, and the source is almost certainly Shinkolobwe.

In October of 2005, a customs official in Tanzania made a routine inspection of a long-haul truck carrying several barrels of a metal called *columbite-tantalite*, otherwise known as coltan, a rare metal used in the manufacture of laptop computers and cell phones and other electronic goods. But he found a lode of unfamiliar black grit instead.

One of his bosses later recalled the scene to a reporter: "There were several containers due to be shipped and they were all routinely scanned with a Geiger counter. This one was very radioactive. When we opened the container it was full of drums of coltan. Each drum contains about fifty kilograms of ore. When the first and second rows were removed, the ones after that were found to be drums of uranium." A United Nations panel came in to investigate and concluded the source of both shipments had been illegal mining at Shinkolobwe.

The clandestine mining of uranium is not hard to conceal in the midst of so much other petty corruption. In most of Union Minière's abandoned pits, there is an active hunt for what is called "Congo caviar"–the rich mineral blend of cobalt and copper harvested by scavengers and purchased by speculators. This activity is supposed to be illegal, but it has been widely tolerated for more than a decade. The miners work in T-shirts and flip-flops and dig out the chunks of caviar with shovels, picks and their bare hands. Approximately 50,000 to 70,000 people are doing this on any given day. The cobalt is particularly prized and fetches high prices. It is a vital metal in the construction of jet engines and turbines. Energy-hungry China is a primary buyer. But in the majority of cases the minerals leave the country illegally, without being recorded and without being taxed. The usual route is through Zambia. And at every step in this unofficial process, from the mine to the border, successive layers of police and inspectors demand a cut.

A common joke among nuclear policy analysts is that the best way to move an atomic bomb across a national border would be to hide it inside a truckload of marijuana. In other words, smuggling routes used by average criminals provide good cover for the occasional piece of nuclear merchandise.

Fueled by a rising worldwide interest in nuclear power, the price of uranium soared in 2007 and in the rush to put old fields back into production, a company called Brinkley Mining signed an agreement in 2007 with the Democratic Republic of Congo for the exploration and exploitation of Shinkolobwe, where the supply of uranium seemed to be bottomless.

As a bonus to the Congo–and perhaps a sign of eagerness–Brinkley also pledged to help fix the dilapidated nuclear reactor in Kinshasa and install radiation detectors to keep stolen uranium from leaving the country.

The deal soon fell apart. Police in Congo arrested two of Kinshasa's top nuclear officials and accused them of conspiring in a criminal plot to illegally export the country's uranium. The pair were released from jail within the week, though kept under investigation. A deputy mining minister said the leases were invalid. "Uranium is a reserved mineral," he told a reporter. "We want to leave it for future generations."

The mystery of the illicit buying continued. There was no accounting of how many bags of uranium might have left Shinkolobwe under a truck tarp and smuggled through Zambia to places unknown. A few Western diplomats suggested that purchasing agents for Iran may have been the ultimate buyers. It might also have been elements of the A.Q. Khan sales network, or terrorists looking for shrapnel in a dirty bomb.

A more banal possibility, and one more likely than any of these, is that it was simply hoarded up by a speculator waiting for a buyer to come forward, much as the Belgian company had patiently awaited a visit from the U.S. Army in the 1940s. The uranium could not be fashioned into a weapon all by itself, but it might be useful to a state with nuclear ambitions. The purloined ore could be fed into a graphite-moderated heavy water reactor, such as those now located at Khushab in Pakistan or Arak in Iran, or even Cirrus in India, which can run on natural uranium. Though this would be a cheaper path to a bomb than conventional enrichment, such a scheme would require a campus that would be hard to conceal from spy satellites. At a minimum, there would have to be a yellowcake mill, a fuel fabrication plant, a reactor and a sophisticated reprocessing shop with glove boxes, precision gear and tubs of nitric acid. A nation which attempted such a cut-rate Manhattan Project would face formidable barriers. They would need millions of dollars and the unpredictable factor of luck. But seventy years of history has shown that nations are willing to make extraordinary sacrifices and challenge long odds to enter the club of the privileged. Nine nations have made the journey thus far.

If a speculator did take a flier in black-market uranium from Shinkolobwe, it would not be difficult to hide it from prying eyes. It could be barreled and stacked in an obscure corner of an industrial yard. It could be stored in a row of tin sheds in a forest. For that matter, it could simply be piled out in the open air, with the perfect disguise as a gravel heap. Rain or snow will not harm it. And its fissile potency will not substantially diminish until approximately seven hundred million years have passed.

After about two hours, we came to the ruins of a metal fence nearly covered in the jacaranda trees on the side of the road. There were a few bricks scattered about. It felt like we were walking through the leavings of a bygone civilization – a garrison on the Roman frontier, perhaps, or one of the forgotten silver villas in the Andes. But this was antiquity of the atomic age.

We walked about a kilometer down a concrete road, past mounds of black dirt, old slag. This was the outer fringe of what had been the "B Zone," the heart of the uranium mining operation run by the Belgians. Shards of iron pipe and green chips of oxidizing copper lay scattered on the path. To the west were the metal skeletons of what had been a warehouse and a water tower.

When we passed though a gap in the trees, a panorama suddenly opened. Across a wide clearing in the forest, it was possible to see a line of trees a mile away, across a low man-made canyon whose sides were stained black and brown and whose bottom held pools of cloudy green water. This was the Shinkolobwe pit, the womb of the atomic bomb. On a different side of the world, a quarter-million Japanese people had been killed with the material from this cavity. There were no freelance miners anywhere in sight, but the soil in the center of the pit had been thoroughly worked over. Broken wood slats were littered about the slopes, the remnants of jerry-built mine works.

The three of us stood at the edge of the pit and looked in for a while. None of us spoke. A few fat cumulus clouds drifted overhead.

We were there for several minutes before I realized that I still had the "letter of authorization" from the police official in my backpack. I hadn't needed to withdraw it because we hadn't encountered a single roadblock. Nobody was guarding Shinkolobwe. We had walked right in.

Spent Nuclear Fuel: A Trash Heap Deadly for 250,000 Years or a Renewable Energy Source?

By David Biello

A 98-foot-wide, two-mile-long ditch with steep walls 33 feet deep that bristles with magnets and radar reflectors will stand for millennia as a warning to future humans not to trifle with what is hidden inside the Waste Isolation Pilot Project (WIPP) outside Carlsbad, N.M. Paired with 48 stone or concrete 105-ton markers, etched with warnings in seven languages ranging from English to Navajo as well as human faces contorted into expressions of horror, the massive installation is meant to stand for at least 10,000 years–twice as long as the Egyptian pyramids have survived.

But the plutonium ensconced in the salt mine at the center of this installation will be lethal to humans for at least 25 times that long–even once the salt walls ooze inward to entomb the legacy of American atomic weapons. And WIPP will only hold a fraction, though a more deadly fraction, of the amount of nuclear waste the U.S. plans to store at Yucca Mountain in Nevada or some other site designated to replace it as a permanent repository for the residue of nuclear reactions.

The Desert Space Foundation, an arts group in Las Vegas, Nev., sponsored a contest to come up with a similar warning system for that site. The winner: genetically-modified yucca cacti turned cobalt blue that would be planted across the entire Yucca Mountain site–to serve as a warning to future civilizations of the radioactive waste within the mountain fastness.

But eerie blue cacti or massive monoliths in the desert may attract rather than repel future explorers–the warnings of the Egyptians did little to deter modern archaeologists. There already are those who see what would be hidden inside Yucca as a resource rather than a curse–after all, as much as 95 percent of the energy in fissile uranium remains in the waste. "The majority of the energy is still in the spent fuel," says Rod McCullum, director of the Yucca Mountain project at the Nuclear Energy Institute (NEI), an industry group. "With Yucca Mountain, you can pull [the nuclear waste] out and reprocess it."

Lonely Mountain

In 1987 Congress passed legislation that required the Department of Energy (DoE) to take possession of and properly store the spent fuel from the nation's 104 nuclear reactors by the then far-off date of February 1998. Now 11 years behind schedule, the DoE's primary response–to bury it deep within Yucca Mountain–is no closer to being a permanent solution.

The Energy Department last June finally applied to the U.S. Nuclear Regulatory Commission (NRC), the federal government agency that oversees the nation's nuclear power plants, for a license to build the repository at Yucca. But taxpayers still spend roughly $1 billion a year (in fines paid by the federal government) to utilities to compensate them for the delay.

All told, the nuclear reactors in the U.S. produce more than 2,000 metric tons of radioactive waste a year, according to the DoE–and most of it ends up sitting on-site because there is nowhere else to put it. "When we remove fuel from the core after its final usage, we store it in a pool on site. We have the capacity to store it there for many years," says Bryan Dolan, vice president of nuclear development at Duke Energy Corp., which operates three nuclear power plants in South Carolina. The amount of space required to store it, after all, is "incredibly small."

In fact, the U.S. nuclear industry has produced roughly 64,000 metric tons (one metric ton equals 1.1 U.S. tons) of radioactive used fuel rods in total or, in the words of NEI, enough "to cover a football field about seven yards deep." (Of course, actually concentrating rods this way would set off a nuclear chain reaction.)

The 1987 measure designated Yucca Mountain–a range of volcanic rock 90 miles (160 kilometers) northwest of Las Vegas in a patch of desert near former nuclear weapon testing sites–as the nation's permanent repository for all of its used fuel. Critics, including environmentalists and Nevada residents and politicians, charge the site is unsuitable for a variety of reasons, most notably because of its proximity to fault lines (earthquakes have already damaged some buildings at Yucca Mountain) and because water that flows through its rock may ultimately circulate radioactive waste into the soil or drinking water.

But the federal government has already spent some $11 billion building a kind of reverse mine, a deep shaft bored into the side of the mountain sheathed in stainless steel in which to bury the waste. To complete the repository would require at least $90 billion in total, according to a Bush administration estimate in 2008, and would not come online before 2017 at the earliest.

That far-off goal seems increasingly unlikely. The powerful Nevada Democrat, Senate Majority Leader Harry Reid, is a leading opponent of storing nuclear waste in his home state. Pres. Barack Obama appears to agree. In 2007 Obama, then a junior senator from Illinois, wrote in a letter to Reid and Sen. Barbara Boxer (D–Calif.) noting that "the selection of Yucca Mountain has failed, the time for debate on this site is over, and it is time to start exploring new alternatives for safe, long-term solutions based on sound science."

And on January 5, Reid said in a statement that Obama "reiterated his promise to work with me to prevent the dump from ever being built."

Finding an alternative or figuring out how to make Yucca Mountain work–there is already so much nuclear waste in the U.S. that, according to NRC, if Yucca were already open, by 2010 it would be filled to its statutory limit of 70,000 metric tons–will take up "a significant part of my time and energy," new Secretary of Energy Stephen Chu, a physicist, testified during his Senate confirmation hearing earlier this month. "We do need a plan on how to dispose of that waste safely, over a long period of time."

Back in 1983 the DoE selected eight possible candidates for permanent storage other than Yucca, including the Vacherie salt dome in Louisiana; the Richton and Cypress Creek salt domes in Mississippi; salt beds in Deaf Smith and Swisher counties, both in Texas; as well as Davis and Lavender canyons in Utah; and the volcanic basalt beneath Hanford, Wash. Other suggested alternatives have included burying the radioactive waste at sea or shooting it into space.

But the federal government has spent more than two decades developing Yucca, leaving it the readiest candidate for a permanent repository. In its absence, the DoE continues to pay fines to the various nuclear power plants around the country for not providing storage for their waste–and the spent nuclear fuel piles up.

Spent Fuel

At present, the nation's nuclear facilities store spent fuel on-site in pools or dry casks. "Our agency is on record as being confident that fuel can be stored safely on-site at reactors in either pools or dry casks for at least 90 years," says David McIntyre, an NRC spokesman.

The glowing nuclear fuel rods rest beneath 40 feet (12 meters) of pale blue water (laced with boron to block stray neutrons, the uncharged atomic particles that initiate a nuclear reaction) and slowly decay for a decade or more. New reactors will be built with at least 18 years worth of spent fuel storage capacity, according to Ed Cummins, vice president of regulatory affairs and standardization at nuclear reactor–maker Westinghouse Electric Co. "The earliest plants are expected in 2015, so you're at 2033" before any additional steps–such as shipping the spent fuel to a repository–would need to be taken.

But nearly all of the nuclear power plants in the U.S. have already run out of storage space, because these pools were not designed to be long-term containers and enough room needs to be preserved in case of a crisis such as a meltdown. In the absence of a long-term solution (such as burying the waste deep inside Yucca Mountain), the nuclear industry has turned to so-called dry cask storage.

This involves immersing the radioactive used rods in helium or some other inert gas and slotting them into a steel container that is further encased in a concrete cask–at a cost of roughly $1 million per cask. The encased rods still manage to emit roughly one millirem of radiation per hour and heat the outside of the 100-plus ton concrete casing to as much as 90 degrees Fahrenheit (32 degrees Celsius).

"These are placed in rows on a concrete pad for stability. They're essentially out in the air," says NRC's McIntyre. "Generally, they are putting them within the controlled area of the reactor site so they are protected under the physical security of the plant."

Some 9,000 metric tons of spent fuel rods are already stored encased in some 900 such casks–the bulk of them stored vertically in concrete casks but some placed horizontally into concrete bunkers. Their makers–companies like New Jersey-based Holtec International and AREVA's Transnuclear, Inc.–and the NRC maintain that such dry cask storage will last for at least a century, if not longer. "They've had an excellent safety record over the past 22 years they've been in use," McIntyre says. "All signs are that they are safe and secure."

But some environmentalists and other nuclear power critics contend that such dry casks present a tempting target for terrorists and a disaster for the environment if ever breached. In fact, the San Luis Obispo, Calif., chapter of Mothers for Peace has successfully sued the NRC and power utility Pacific Gas & Electric Co.–owners of the Diablo Canyon power plant–for failing to take into account the impact of a potential terrorist strike when assessing the environmental risks of a new, proposed on-site dry cask storage area.

The solution may be one or many interim storage sites, centralized depots where such dry casks could be stored until a permanent repository is opened. Eleven communities in Idaho, Illinois, Kentucky, New Mexico, Ohio, South Carolina, Tennessee and Washington State have expressed an interest in being the host of such a facility, according to NEI. "It should be wherever it can be sited and it should be at a voluntary location," NEI's McCullum says. "Anything that is on the way to Yucca Mountain from most of the reactors," which are in the eastern half of the U.S.

Recycling

In 1972 General Electric Co. closed a building in Morris, Ill., that would have presented another alternative solution to the problem of nuclear waste: reprocessing. The U.S. government originally employed this technology–dubbed PUREX (for plutonium and uranium recovery by extraction)–in both Barnwell, S.C., and West Valley, N.Y., to separate out the plutonium and other reusable fission products from nuclear waste. Today, France, Japan, Russia and the U.K. have reprocessing facilities that extract fresh fuel by enriching spent nuclear rods–albeit also producing radioactive waste by-products that have to be dumped.

The problem is that this is also how governments separate out plutonium for use in nuclear weapons–potentially creating a tempting target for theft. "One of the biggest obstacles to increasing security is the proliferation of reprocessing plants, which produce separated plutonium that can be used in weapons," says physicist Edwin Lyman, a senior staff scientist at the Union of Concerned Scientists (UCS), a nonprofit that advocates for a healthy environment and safer world. "We do not think any reprocessing scheme existing or proposed can mitigate the serious concern of proliferation and nuclear terrorism." Some 250 metric tons of plutonium–enough for 30,000 nuclear weapons–has already been reprocessed by the aforementioned countries, according to the group.

The Bush administration revived interest in such reprocessing via the Global Nuclear Energy Partnership (GNEP) in 2006. This DoE program proposes restarting the recycling of nuclear fuel in the U.S. by building a new reprocessing plant, which prompted GE to reopen the Morris, Ill., site, among other companies stepping forward. At the same time, the Energy Department has enlisted 21 nations, from Australia to Kazakhstan, to safely develop such reprocessing technology, in many cases by shipping any future spent fuel to this proposed U.S. facility.

The National Research Council, the research arm of the U.S. National Academy of Sciences, notes, however, that such reprocessing is impractical and expensive. In 1996 it estimated that reprocessing of existing used nuclear fuel could cost more than $100 billion. Eleven years later, the Council further declared that research and development of such technology under the GNEP should be halted, because the money could be better spent on other areas of nuclear power research, such as next-generation reactors.

The nuclear power industry has also not shown much enthusiasm for reprocessing because of the high price tag. "This GNEP program is aimed at trying to understand whether you could reprocess spent fuel economically," says Westinghouse's Cummins. "I would suggest that it is not really economical."

A 2007 report issued by a Colorado think tank, The Keystone Center–an analysis of nuclear power by utility executives, environmentalists, policymakers and other experts–agrees, finding that "reprocessing of spent fuel will not be cost-effective in the foreseeable future."

"Commercial spent fuel has plutonium in it and you can think of that as an ore that could be mined for fissile material," Lyman notes. But "the cost of extracting plutonium from that ore is still much, much higher than the price of uranium."

Nevertheless, advocates including researchers at Idaho, Argonne, Los Alamos and Oak Ridge national laboratories point to a reprocessing future of so-called fast-breeder reactors, which use plutonium to generate electricity–and in the process of fissioning generate yet more plutonium, a theoretically inexhaustible source of energy. "In theory, it could produce a self-sustaining energy supply," Lyman acknowledges. "But in practice it's never worked."

In fact, the Monju fast-breeder reactor in Tsuruga on Japan's west coast was shut down in 1995 after slightly more than a year of operation because of political opposition and difficulties running it, including a fire caused by a leak of its liquid sodium coolant, despite a cost of more than $6 billion to build. "Breeders are difficult reactors, they are complex reactors," Westinghouse's Cummins says. "There have been some built but not many more. They are just not economical at the moment."

And even if reprocessing or fast breeders could be made to work cheaply and efficiently–eliminating spent reactor rods as radioactive refuse–there would still be thousands of tons of nuclear waste in need of a permanent home.

The Other Nuclear Waste

The U.S. produces as much as 160,000 cubic feet (4,530 cubic meters) of radioactive material from its nuclear power plants annually–a number that spikes higher dramatically when old nuclear plants are decommissioned, such as Maine Yankee in Wiscasset, Me., in 1997. Ranging from workers' coveralls to water filters, some of this stream of nuclear waste no longer has a place for its disposal either–particularly the highly radioactive materials rated as classes B and C, such as reactor vessel heads. "That stuff has only one place it can go," says Ralph Andersen, chief health physicist at NEI, "a deep geologic repository," like Yucca Mountain.

The national nuclear dump in Barnwell, S.C., was closed to shipments of such waste from nuclear power plants in 36 states in July 2008. A new dump in Texas, granted a license by the state this month, will only accept low-level leavings from that state and Vermont, alongside similarly restricted dumps in Utah and Washington State. This has also left users of nuclear products such as hospitals and universities scrambling to find a place to dispose of their radioactive residue.

So now the waste from the majority of reactors on the east coast and Midwest typically sits alongside the spent nuclear fuel in dry casks on-site. In terms of safety, it's the best that can be done at present.

"Where would I want to store radioactive materials? Somewhere where there were armed security officers with concrete buildings," Andersen says. "What we've got at a nuclear power plant is an armed fortress made out of concrete."

About the Author

David Biello is a contributing editor at Scientific American.

Abandoned Uranium Mines: An "Overwhelming Problem" in the Navajo Nation

By Francie Diep

There's an old uranium mine on rancher Larry Gordy's grazing land near Cameron, Ariz. Like hundreds of other abandoned mines in the Navajo Nation, the United States' largest Indian reservation, it looks as if it might still be in use–tailings, or waste products of uranium processing, are still piled everywhere, and the land isn't fenced off. "It looks like Mars," said Marsha Monestersky, program director of Forgotten People, an advocacy organization for the western region of the vast Navajo Nation, which covers 27,000 square miles in Arizona, Utah and New Mexico.

The U.S. Environmental Protection Agency is currently embroiled in a massive effort to assess 520 open abandoned uranium mines all over the vast reservation. (Forgotten People says there are even more mines on Navajo land: about 1,300.) Earlier this month, the cleanup got a boost from a bankruptcy settlement with Oklahoma City-based chemical company Tronox Inc., which will give federal and Navajo Nation officials $14.5 million to address the reservation's uranium contamination.

During the Cold War, private companies such as Tronox's former parent company, Kerr-McGee Corp., operated uranium mines under U.S. government contracts, removing four million tons of ore that went into making nuclear weapons and fuel. When demand dried up with the end of the era, companies simply abandoned their mines as they were.

Remediation work started 10 years ago, when the EPA mapped the mines by investigating company records and surveying the land with helicopters equipped with radiation detectors. The agency is now halfway through visiting mines to determine their radiation levels. "It's an overwhelming problem," said Clancy Tenley, EPA assistant director for the region.

The mines expose Navajo Nation residents to uranium through airborne dust and contaminated drinking water. Many residents' homes were built using mud and rocks near mines, and some of that building material is radioactive. There are few published studies on the effects of uranium mines on nearby residents, but researchers at the Centers for Disease Control and Prevention and the University of New Mexico are working on health assessments, according to EPA officials. Researchers have known for decades that uranium exposure increases the risk of lung and bone cancers and kidney damage.

In July, the leaders of Forgotten People pushed the EPA to begin cleanup in Cameron because they were worried about the effects of the mines there on ranchers like Gordy, whose cattle drink and graze on uranium-contaminated land. Their tussle with the agency highlights the difficulties the EPA faces in all stages of its cleanup, which will likely take decades. The uranium mine Gordy found wasn't even included in the EPA's original atlas. "We're grateful to [Monestersky] for pointing that out to us," said Tenley, the agency spokesman. He initially said the EPA would visit the site within six months but publicity over conditions there apparently prompted a change of heart.

Instead, EPA contractors assessed the site November 9. A scientist who participated wouldn't discuss what he found without EPA officials present, and agency officials couldn't be reached for comment. However, Lee Greer, a biologist from La Sierra University in Riverside, Calif., was part of a conference call about the assessment's results. Greer has been working with Forgotten People to record radiation levels at sites that interest the advocacy group. He said the EPA contractors found radiation levels at the mine that were higher than the EPA's Geiger counters could measure.

The accelerated assessment of Gordy's ranch came six days after Greer presented his radiation results from the site to the Geological Society of America. A geologist who was present at the society meeting said that, based on Greer's findings, a cleanup of the mine should be a high priority. "The sooner, the better," said Michael Phillips, a professor at Illinois Valley Community College. Because the uranium at this mine is on the surface of the land, people and animals are more likely to come in contact with it, he added.

But the preliminary assessment of the site is just the first step on a long road to a cleanup that is years and possibly even decades away. The time lag between an assessment and a remediation job depends on what scientists find at a particular mine, said Andrew Bain, EPA remediation project manager. The U.S.'s five-year plan for the Navajo Nation's uranium mines only covers assessment, not cleanup. The EPA started remediating the reservation's largest mine, the Northeast Church Rock Mine in New Mexico, in 2005, and doesn't expect to finish until 2019. "We have no estimate for how long it'll take to clean up all the mines," agency spokesman Tenley said.

As for the price tag, the recent Tronox settlement will only cover a fraction of the overall cleanup. Just assessing the uranium mines in the Navajo Nation costs the EPA about $12 million every year, said Tenley. Remediation would cost more, he added. How much more? "In the hundreds of millions," he said.

All this means a long wait for residents like Gordy, though they've already waited more than 20 years since the close of the Cold War. "It's taking forever to get it cleaned up," said Don Yellowman, president of Forgotten People. "It seems like everyone's aware but nobody's taking notice. We don't understand."

This article is provided by Scienceline, *a project of New York University's Science, Health and Environmental Reporting Program.*

Hanford Nuclear Waste Cleanup Plant May Be Too Dangerous

By Valerie Brown

The most toxic and voluminous nuclear waste in the U.S.–208 million liters–sits in decaying underground tanks at the Hanford Site (a nuclear reservation) in southeastern Washington State. It accumulated there from the middle of World War II, when the Manhattan Project invented the first nuclear weapon, to 1987, when the last reactor shut down. The federal government's current attempt at a permanent solution for safely storing that waste for centuries–the Waste Treatment and Immobilization Plant here–has hit a major snag in the form of potential chain reactions, hydrogen explosions and leaks from metal corrosion. And the revelation last February that six more of the storage tanks are currently leaking has further ramped up the pressure for resolution.

After decades of research, experimentation and political inertia, the U.S. Department of Energy (DoE) started building the "Vit Plant" at Hanford in 2000. It's intended to sequester the waste in stainless steel–encased glass logs, a process known as vitrification (hence "Vit"), so it cannot escape into the environment, barring natural disasters like earthquakes or catastrophic fires. But progress on the plant slowed to a crawl last August, when numerous interested parties acknowledged that the plant's design might present serious safety risks. In response, then-Energy Secretary Steven Chu appointed an expert panel to find a way forward. Because 60 of the 177 underground tanks have already leaked and all are at increasing risk to do so, solving the problem is urgent.

Vitrification Prep 101: Some Tough Homework

The plant's construction, currently contracted by the DoE to Bechtel National, Inc., may be the most complicated engineering project underway in the U.S. But back in 2000 the DoE and Bechtel decided to save time and money by starting construction before crucial structures and processes had been designed and properly tested at a scale comparable to full operation. This wasn't such a good idea, says Dirk Dunning, nuclear material specialist with the Oregon Department of Energy. "The worst possible time to save money is at the beginning. You're better off to be very nearly complete on design before you begin construction."

The vitrification project calls for the waste to be analyzed chemically and radiologically before it enters a pretreatment facility to be separated into various constituents such as cesium 137, strontium 90 and metals. After that, each separate waste stream is channeled as either high-level or low-activity waste into designated melters. The glass is created by mixing sand with a few additives like boron; the waste is stirred in, and the whole mess is melted, then decanted into the steel canisters. After the glass logs solidify, the waste is trapped and should be isolated from the environment for long enough for most of the radioactivity to decay to safe levels.

The low-level waste canisters will be stored permanently at Hanford. Because the planned Yucca Mountain geologic repository project was halted by the Obama administration, the high-level waste canisters will be kept at Hanford in an as-yet unconstructed building. In January the DoE announced it is beginning work on a new "comprehensive management and disposal system" that will make a permanent geologic repository available by 2048. Yet even if all goes perfectly from now on, it will take until 2062 to vitrify all the waste.

The waste presents significant challenges for Vit Plant project engineers and nuclear chemists. For one thing, the waste varies wildly from tank to tank. The former nuclear weapons facility at Savannah River, Ga.–also part of the Manhattan Project–has been successfully vitrifying weapons waste for years, but only one fuel separation process was used there. At Hanford there were nine production reactors making plutonium and uranium fuel using at least six different radiochemical processes whose chemistry, and thus constituents, were very different. This remains true of the waste as well. There are large differences in composition from tank to tank that necessitate chemically profiling the waste in batches before it enters the Vit Plant, which may also require changes to the glass formula at the other end of the process.

Overall, the tanks hold every element in the periodic table, including half a ton of plutonium, various uranium isotopes and at least 44 other radionuclides–containing a total of about 176 million curies of radioactivity. This is almost twice the radioactivity released at Chernobyl, according to *Plutopia: Nuclear Families, Atomic Cities, and the Great Soviet and American Plutonium Disasters*, by Kate Brown, a history professor at the University of Maryland, Baltimore County. The waste is also physically hot as well as laced with numerous toxic and corrosive chemicals and heavy metals that threaten the integrity of the pipes and tanks carrying the waste, risking leakage.

The physical form of the waste causes problems, too. It's very difficult to get a representative sample from any given tank because the waste has settled into layers, starting with a baked-on "hard heal" at the bottom, a layer of salt cake above that, a layer of gooey sludge, then fluid, and finally gases in the headspace between the fluid and the ceiling. Most of the radioactivity is in the solids and sludge whereas most of the volume is in the liquids and the salt cake.

Going with the Flow

All of these considerations contribute to the overall problem, which can be summed up in one word: flow. To get to the glass log stage, the waste has to travel through an immense labyrinth of tanks and pipes. It has to move at a fast enough clip to avoid pipe and filter clogs as well as prevent solids from settling. This is quite a challenge given the multiphasic nature of the waste: solids, liquids, sludge and gases all move differently. The waste feed through the system will be in the form of a "non-Newtonian slurry"–a mixture of fluids and solids of many different shapes, sizes and densities. If the solids stop moving, problems ensue.

For one thing, there's a chance that enough plutonium could congregate to trigger a nuclear chain reaction, or criticality–the self-sustaining cascade of atomic fission that releases massive amounts of energy. That would be a serious event even if an explosion did not breach the concrete containment building. Hot slurry could surge backward through the piping, spreading the problem to other parts of the system. Waste solids could also clog pipes, along with ion-exchange filters designed to grab the most radioactive constituents from the low-level waste for addition to the high-level stream.

Whether the solids pile up in the vessels, the pipes or the filters, says Donna Busche, nuclear and environmental safety manager for Hanford contractor URS Corp., "that's where I've got the problem." Further construction of the Vit Plant's flawed components cannot proceed unless Busche issues an operating permit, which she is loath to do. She calls the DoE's failure to require that Bechtel resolve the safety issues sooner "obscene."

A second explosive risk could arise because both heat and radiation can disassemble water into oxygen and hydrogen. If there are not places along the piping and in the vessels for hydrogen to exit the flow of waste, enough could build up to explode.

And then there's the extreme radioactivity of the waste, which is far too high for direct human exposure. Enter the Vit Plant's notorious "black cells." These are 18 massive concrete enclosures populated by smaller stainless steel vessels. The idea is to guide the waste through the vessels without any human intervention over the 40 years officials believe it will take to process all the waste. The only way to do this is to ensure that the black cells have no moving parts. But because the waste has to be constantly stirred to prevent settling of the noxious and radioactive solids, the plan calls for pulse jet mixers–described as "turkey basters"–to keep the solids suspended.

The pulse jet mixers suck waste into their vertical tubes and then eject it forcefully back into the tanks. Unfortunately, they have not yet been shown to provide sufficient mixing at the scale necessary for the Vit Plant. They do, however, apply enough force to the slurry for the solids to grind away at the stainless steel of tanks and pipes, weakening them enough to risk leakage. Besides this erosion, there's also potential for chemical corrosion. The Defense Nuclear Safety Board, which advises the White House, has called these problems "a show-stopper."

"The way [the plant] is currently designed poses unacceptable risks. DoE now admits that," says Tom Carpenter, executive director of the watchdog group Hanford Challenge. In December the Government Accountability Office issued a highly critical analysis of the Vit Plant's unresolved safety issues

Disagreements over the safety risks have also prompted outspoken protests from several senior Hanford officials. Chief project engineer Gary Brunson resigned in January. Busche and former deputy chief process engineer Walter Tamosaitis filed whistleblower complaints alleging that their concerns about safety were suppressed by Bechtel. (Bechtel declined to be interviewed for this story, citing nondisclosure agreements signed with Chu's expert panel.)

But Langdon Holton, DoE's senior technical authority for the Vit Plant and a member of Chu's expert panel, believes the project's problems are technical snags, rather than the insoluble consequence of incompetence or hubris. He also thinks that although the current risks are real, they are unlikely and would be of low magnitude if they did occur. For example, he says, "You'd have to have a vessel unmixed for half a year" for enough hydrogen to accumulate for a significant explosion. "Do I have concern we won't be able to resolve the issues? No, but it will take some time," he adds. (Chu's panel does not expect to issue a formal report, according to Holton.)

Time may be limited. The 177 tanks, built between 1943 and 1986 and most intended for only about a 20-year life span, are decaying; at last count, six are leaking. The Vit Plant was supposed to start operating in 2007 and is now projected to begin in 2022. Its original budget was $4.3 billion and is now estimated at $13.4 billion. Nobody is suggesting the project be abandoned, yet forging ahead without confidence in the plant's safe operation is not really an option either. The real question, many Hanford watchers say, is whether the country wants to pay for doing it right.

Busche is adamant that the safety issues must be solved before plans proceed further. "The level of robustness we have to put in all our systems is derived from the waste itself," she says. "It's the gift that keeps giving until it's in a glass log."

Nuclear Waste Is Piling Up. Does the U.S. Have a Plan?

By Allison Macfarlane & Rodney C. Ewing

As small modular nuclear reactors come closer to reality in the U.S., managing and disposing of their highly radioactive waste should be a national priority. Forty years after the passage of the Nuclear Waste Policy Act, there is, "no clear path forward for the siting, licensing, and construction of a geologic repository" for nuclear waste, according to a recent U.S. National Academies of Science, Engineering and Medicine report.

The good news is that there is already a clear strategy for managing and disposing of this highly radioactive material. The bad news is that the U.S. government has yet to seriously follow that plan.

The National Academies report tells us that new or advanced reactor designs–the hoped-for saviors of the nuclear industry–will not save us from the need to build geologic repositories, deep-mined facilities for permanent nuclear waste disposal. In some cases, these new reactors may make it worse by creating more waste that's more costly to manage, new kinds of complex waste, or just more waste, period. Before we face that onrush, we first need to deal with the large volume of waste we've already produced.

The U.S., which led the way on managing nuclear waste in the 1980s and 1990s, has now fallen to the back of the pack. About 88,000 metric tons of spent nuclear fuel from commercial reactors remain stranded at reactor sites, and this number is increasing by some 2,000 metric tons each year. These 77 sites are in 35 states and threaten to become de facto permanent disposal facilities. Without a geologic repository, there is no way forward for the final disposal of this highly radioactive material. Storing it in pools and dry casks at reactor sites is a temporary solution; it is safe for decades, but not the millennia needed to isolate this radioactive material from the environment. The present U.S. policy of indefinite storage at a centralized site is not a viable solution, as it shifts the cost and risk to future generations.

Beginning now, the nation needs to follow a pathway already set out for a national nuclear waste repository. Both a 2012 presidential Blue Ribbon Commission and an international expert panel organized by Stanford and George Washington Universities in 2018 recommended a new, independent waste management and disposal organization with funding outside of the annual Congressional appropriations and restrictive budgetary rules. The Blue Ribbon Commission called for creation of a new federal corporation, like the Tennessee Valley Authority, for this organization, while the Stanford/GWU panel looked to replicate not-for-profit, utility-owned, but independent, organizations modeled on successful programs in other countries, such as Sweden and Finland. Charges to nuclear-power-produced electricity fund these organizations, and they remain regulated by independent nuclear regulators. Both panels agreed on the need for an independent organization and finances.

Nations that followed this blueprint are now addressing their nuclear waste problem. Sweden's SKB nonprofit announced last year that it will build a deep geologic repository at Östhammar for the permanent disposal of spent fuel from its commercial nuclear reactors. In Finland, construction of a geologic repository began in May 2021, with plans to accept spent nuclear fuel by the mid-2020s. The Nordic countries are not the only ones making progress: France, Canada and Switzerland are all pushing toward license applications to begin construction.

A U.S. waste management organization must be a trusted and capable agency that is well-funded and staffed. Sweden's SKB sustained decades of effort on both public engagement and technical analysis around siting and now is reaping the benefits. The U.S. Department of Energy, the designated repository implementer established by the Nuclear Waste Policy Act, instead suffers from leadership and priorities that change with each administration, as well as a history of broken promises that have led to little public confidence that it is up to the job.

The overwhelming majority of successful repository programs overseas are run by independent corporations established by the nuclear industry–outside government. The industry is best positioned to manage the back end of the nuclear fuel cycle, from discharge of spent fuel from the reactor, through storage, shipment and final geologic disposal.

Consent from people living nearby is another universal requirement to establish an accepted geologic repository. Different motivations will underpin a community, tribe or state's decision to host one. A municipality may volunteer because of the jobs that will last over the long life of the project (probably over 100 years) or improvements in roads, schools or other infrastructure. Some may feel the need to contribute to the greater good of society, especially if they benefited from the electricity produced by nuclear power, as is the case in Sweden.

The 2012 Blue Ribbon Commission suggested that communities should decide for themselves what consent looks like to ensure a successful repository decision. Indeed, Canada is following this approach. The two finalist communities in its siting process will handle the decision differently, one by referendum, the other by elected council decision.

Affected communities will need resources to hire their own experts to validate claims made by the designated nuclear waste management agency. Sweden, in fact, not only provided such funds, but also money for public interest groups that opposed the repository, as part of the effort to produce a compelling safety case for Östhammar.

Assured finances are also key. In the U.S., Congress hasn't appropriated funds for its Yucca Mountain nuclear waste program since 2010. In fact, Congress has so badly mangled the process of collecting and appropriating the ratepayers fund, now over $40 billion, that it has rendered these funds essentially inaccessible. Outrageously, this money, actually collected from electricity ratepayers, not taxpayers, is being used to offset the national debt.

Even if the U.S. starts today, it will take decades to site, design and build a facility for disposal of its nuclear waste stockpile. That process must accelerate now, before the reactors we need for their electricity run out of room for their growing inventories of highly radioactive waste.

This is an opinion and analysis article, and the views expressed by the author or authors are not necessarily those of Scientific American.

About the Authors

Allison Macfarlane is director of the School of Public Policy and Global Affairs at the University of British Columbia and former chairman of the U.S. Nuclear Regulatory Commission.

Rodney C. Ewing is co-director of the Center for International Security and Cooperation at Stanford University and former chairman of the U.S. Nuclear Waste Technical Review Board.

Section 6: Nuclear Weapons

Behind the Scenes at a U.S. Factory Building New Nuclear Bombs

By Sarah Scoles

Within every American nuclear weapon sits a bowling-ball-size sphere of the strangest element on the planet. This sphere, called a plutonium pit, is the bomb's central core. It's surrounded by conventional explosives. When those explosives blow, the plutonium is compressed, and its atoms begin to split, releasing radiation and heating the material around it. The reaction ignites the sequence of events that makes nuclear weapons nuclear.

In early nuclear bombs, like the ones the U.S. dropped on Japan in World War II, the fission of plutonium or uranium and the fatal energy released were the end of the story. In modern weapons, plutonium fission ignites a second, more powerful stage in which hydrogen atoms undergo nuclear fusion, releasing even more energy. The U.S. hasn't made these pits in a significant way since the late 1980s.

But that is changing. The country is modernizing its nuclear arsenal, making upgrades to old weapons and building new ones. The effort includes updated missiles, a new weapon design, alterations to existing designs and new pits. To accomplish the last item, the National Nuclear Security Administration has enacted a controversial plan to produce 50 new pits a year at the Savannah River Site in South Carolina and 30 pits a year at Los Alamos National Laboratory in New Mexico, the birthplace of the bomb. The first pits will be designed for a weapon called W87-1, which will tip the new intercontinental ballistic missile, called Sentinel. After that the complex will produce pits for other bomb designs.

Not everyone believes this work is necessary. Pit production foments controversy because it's costly and potentially risky and because the existing pits might still work for a while. The physics of plutonium is complex, and no one knows when the original pits will expire. The details of how the pits are made and how they work are among America's most closely guarded secrets. Yet in June 2023 Los Alamos officials invited a group of journalists to tour the facility for the first time in years.

We were there as the lab and the broader National Nuclear Security Administration Complex were embarking on a charm offensive to support the new plutonium work. They have to win over the tax-paying public and recruit some 2,500 new employees for the job. Some of those workers must do high-hazard work that requires expertise the country has largely let slip since the last days of the cold war. Back then, many thought the world was heading toward disarmament, and the skills necessary for a nuclear resurgence seemed unlikely to be called for. That's not quite what happened. Instead China is rapidly growing its nuclear arsenal, and Russia, at war with Ukraine, touts new missile tests and its own nuclear modernization. The U.S. is doing the same. The world order feels fragile; the renewed focus on nuclear weapons threatens to create a 21st-century arms race and an increased reliance on the shaky peace that nuclear weapons may or may not help keep.

Much of the plutonium work at Los Alamos takes place in a building called PF-4, which is located south of town in a part of the lab complex called Tech Area 55. It is one of the most highly guarded parts of the lab. Before our tour, we're told to survey our hands, forearms and ankles for scrapes or scratches into which radioactive contamination could slip. Onto these abrasions we're instructed to place technical protection: Band-Aids. The message is repeated within the building by a sign that instructs those entering to "occlude your wound."

A jarring mix of upbeat friendliness and deadly seriousness greets us at the facility. A cheerful wood sign outside the building welcomes visitors, and security guards fist-bump as we walk in. But those same guards wear long guns, and their eyes swivel tightly as we pass through a TSA-like portal into the bowels of the building. A security force will follow the group—who have been parted from phones, cameras and recorders, as well as all metal, nylon and polyester—the entire afternoon.

Once we're past the initial screening, we step into an airlock with yellow doors on either side of a capsular room. Only one door can be open at a time to keep potential radiological contaminants trapped within PF-4. After we pass through without setting off the alarm, we put on anticontamination lab coats–color-coded red for visitors without security clearance and yellow for the people who belong here. We scrunch disposable booties over our shoes (the security guards get camo shoe covers). Safety goggles slip over our faces, and radiation badges are clipped to our fronts, measuring the invisible energy and particles that whip through them. All plutonium work has been paused for the day to conceal the classified details of pit production.

Element 94, as plutonium is also known, is rare. Dying stars produce a small amount during their last, hot gasps, but that star stuff had decayed nearly out of existence before Earth formed. The planet has made a bit of its own: in what is now Gabon, Africa, algae concentrated natural uranium over the eons, forming a natural fission reactor that produced four tons of plutonium. That plutonium, too, has since decayed away. Scientists inferred the existence of the natural nuclear reactions from the ratio of uranium isotopes that were left in modern times.

The plutonium used for weapons exists only because people made it. In 1940 scientists used a particle accelerator at the University of California, Berkeley, to bombard an isotope of uranium (which has 92 protons per atom) with nuclei of deuterium (a proton and a neutron stuck together). That created neptunium (93 protons per atom), which conveniently decayed into plutonium with its 94 protons per atom. Thus, one of the most efficient ingredients for making a nuclear weapon was born. It's easier and cheaper to make enough plutonium for a weapon than it is to produce enough enriched uranium, the only other element used to sustain a fission chain reaction in nuclear weapons. And fission is what achieves the pressures and temperatures necessary to ignite fusion in the secondary part of the bomb.

Plutonium's genesis was repeated in reactors for decades. In fact, scientists made so much that no new plutonium is required for the new pits at Savannah River and Los Alamos—the current supply can be repurposed, reshaped, reborn.

None of those actions, though, will be simple because plutonium is not simple. Joseph Martz, a scientist in Los Alamos's materials science and technology division, has spent his career mapping the specifics of that complication. Martz started working with plutonium while he was still in college, manipulating it within protective glove boxes that shield workers from radiation. He's never forgotten the first time he touched element 94. Even through thick gloves and from behind glass, he could still feel it: the kilogram of material in his hand was warm. "I remember actually being a bit afraid," he says. "I had almost a terror reaction."

Since then, his fear has given way to fascination with the substance. There is plenty to be fascinated by. It's pliable and compliant in some conditions and delicately brittle in others. When it's a liquid, melting around 650 degrees Celsius, it's the most viscous of all the elements, dripping languidly. If you heat it in its solid form, sometimes it expands, and other times it contracts. It's reactive with air, swiftly shifting its appearance from a silvery metal to a rainbow spectrum of tarnish. When it solidifies, it expands, like water, and its length and density change without much provocation. Its most famous trick, of course, is its propensity for radioactive decay, through which it transforms itself out of existence.

This tendency is also what makes it so dangerous. Inhaled plutonium decays in the body, releasing alpha particles (helium nuclei) that can wreak havoc. The isotope plutonium 238, used as a heat and power source but not in weapons, exhibits other strange behaviors. "If you spill it in the laboratory, it will move around on its own," Martz says. The oomph from a plutonium atom's decay sends it shooting across a surface. "It can get everywhere," he adds.

Plutonium's strangeness comes from its arrangement of electrons. The element occupies the part of the periodic table where atoms' "5f subshell" begins to fill. That's relevant to plutonium's behavior because the "f" electrons reside in narrow energy bands that overlap, allowing the electrons to slip between the bands easily. When they do, Martz says, "the nature of those 'f' electrons changes behavior dramatically." Change the temperature, for instance, and some of the electrons bond with nearby atoms "in very complex shapes," Martz says. The combinatorics mean that plutonium comes in six different solid phases, each with its own crystal structure and strange behavior.

It's taken scientists decades to discover all of this. "What we know today to be the complexity of plutonium was not known to the Manhattan Project scientists," Martz says. For years those secret scientists didn't actually have any plutonium to study–it had to be painstakingly produced. "Almost everything was theoretical," says Alan Carr, senior historian at Los Alamos. "In lieu of the actual material, they'd have chalk and chalkboards and notebooks." The first full gram of element 94 arrived on Los Alamos's mesas in April 1944. The substance had already perplexed the researchers. When they took basic measurements of characteristics such as density, they saw huge variations. Eventually they were able to make their first hemispheres of plutonium metal–protoversions of the pits of today, the size of a golf ball. Yet when they came to the lab the next day ready to experiment, they found that the hemispheres had cracked because their properties and dimensions had shifted. "It was maddening," Martz says.

A breakthrough came later in 1944, when one Manhattan Project scientist suggested that combining plutonium with another element to make an alloy might stabilize it in a phase that was workable. The problem was, they didn't know which element might work. According to a historical document Martz discovered, the scientists had a very scientific method for deciding what substances to try: "Whatever we found in the cupboard," they wrote. Eventually they discovered that gallium did the trick. It's still used in pits today.

In the excitement of these early scientific discoveries, the point of the work would sometimes get lost: it was all in the service of creating a deadly superweapon. In 1945 the U.S. dropped a uranium fission bomb on Hiroshima and then sent a plutonium bomb–essentially a pit encased in explosives–to devastate Nagasaki. The bombs killed tens of thousands of people immediately and more after the fact.

As Manhattan Project physicist I. I. Rabi had feared, according to a quotation in the 2005 book *American Prometheus*, "the culmination of three centuries of physics" was a weapon of mass destruction.

Soon after the war, production of plutonium pits migrated to a facility outside Boulder, Colo. Called Rocky Flats, it could churn out thousands of pits a year—a level of productivity perhaps enabled by its violation of environmental regulations, which in 1989 resulted in a federal raid and then a permanent shutdown. "The public wasn't considered at the time," says Bob Webster, deputy director of weapons at Los Alamos. Not long after, as a result of a testing moratorium and treaty, the country's nuclear weapons complex underwent another phase shift. Scientists and engineers had always tested weapons in the easiest way possible: by blowing them up. If they exploded as expected, officials froze the design and made more clones of that weapon. The researchers never had a true understanding of why everything worked or what might cause it not to—or of how both those things might change over time.

But in 1992 President George H. W. Bush announced a moratorium on nuclear testing. Sig Hecker, at the time director of Los Alamos and now a professor at Stanford University, was in Washington, D.C., when he heard the announcement. "I came back to Los Alamos and told our people, 'Look, the world has just changed,'" he says. They were going to have to maintain the stockpile by understanding its physics without testing it. That task has proved particularly complicated for the plutonium pits, which are all now decades old. Because plutonium was first synthesized only 80 years ago, no one's been able to observe how it behaves as its life wears on past that point.

How aging affects a pit is the subject of contention, but some things are certain: As the plutonium atoms in a pit decay, their products damage the crystal structure of the plutonium that remains, creating voids and defects. These decays also contaminate the pit with helium, americium, uranium and neptunium, among other things. In 50 years a kilogram of plutonium will amass around 0.2 liter of helium. As pits change, their performance and safety in any conditions—including just sitting on a shelf—become questionable.

Pavel Podvig, a senior researcher at the United Nations Institute for Disarmament Research and a researcher with the Program on Science and Global Security at Princeton University, who has questioned the motivation for modernization, concedes, "If you maintain the arsenal, at some point it would be safer to have new pits."

Scientists still don't know the lifetime of a plutonium pit. JASON—a clandestine group of scientists that provides advice for the government—first projected in 2007 that the pits would last decades longer, implying no production program was necessary. But it changed its stance in 2019, stating, "We urge that pit manufacturing be re-established as expeditiously as possible in parallel with the focused program to understand [plutonium] aging." The National Nuclear Security Administration's own studies have suggested the pits will last at least 150 years but also that their degradation could result in surprise defects. And scientists may never know exactly what those defects do or how they would affect an explosion because the ostensible point of nuclear weapons is to never use them.

So far restarting American pit production is proving challenging. Los Alamos's efforts are at least a year behind schedule, and Savannah River's are more like five years delayed.

The Defense Nuclear Facilities Safety Board and other critics have claimed that PF-4 isn't resilient enough against the kind of earthquake geologists now know could occur in Los Alamos. Such significant shaking and the fires it could cause, the board alleged at a hearing last year, could result in plutonium contamination that reaches the public. Inside PF-4 our tour group encounters a poster laying out the lab's Seismic Analysis of Facilities and Evaluation of Risk, also known as SAFER, a program that has resulted in upgrades to the building itself and the equipment within. In 2022 the safety board deemed this modernization to be still not quite good enough.

Some at the lab disagree, including Matt Johnson, head of pit production, who's leading us through PF-4. "If there is an earthquake, this is where I want to be," he says, gazing at the poster. Other safety concerns have come up recently, though. In May the National Nuclear Security Administration released an investigation about four 2021 incidents: one criticality safety violation, one breach that resulted in skin contamination for three workers, and two flooding events that sent water toward fissionable materials. The agency determined that the contractor that manages Los Alamos had violated safety, procedural, management and quality-assurance rules.

Webster, also on the tour in his official yellow lab coat, says the lab and its workers take safety seriously but admits problems are inevitable. "We will always have issues at the lowest level," he says. If everything started going perfectly, he says, they would lower the limit of what counts as a safety violation so people would still get practice reporting. But, he notes, the cutoff is already low: "Rooms would get shut down if they were as radioactive as Fiestaware."

Those rooms, dedicated to various parts of the pit-production enterprise, all have one thing in common: they're full of glove boxes, the radiation-protective equipment inside which workers manipulate plutonium. Long gloves are sealed to openings in glass so sheathed hands can touch samples safely. The gloves themselves have dates written on them so workers know when to replace them. Everyone wears two pairs. The glass windows are surrounded by a metal box that looks like it could be made of plutonium: dull silver with smooth, rounded corners, which are easier to clean and harder for particles to lodge in. "You could eat off this," Webster says. "Not in here," he adds.

On the tour, we are forbidden from setting our notebooks down lest potential contamination stick to them. Should we drop them, a radiological control technician—who has been following us the whole time and scans our hands and feet for radioactivity anytime we leave a room—would measure each page before returning them.

In some places the glove box windows are covered by aluminum foil, blocking classified material from our view. Above these boxes, in every room, there is a kind of trolley system that workers use to move plutonium from room to room. In some rooms, radioactive waste is packaged and waiting to go to a storage facility, with the dosage one might receive from standing near it written on the ground. We are never allowed to forget that this is a dangerous place.

The workers who make pits face these risks every day. To do their jobs, they must first recover and purify plutonium from the old material. Then they "cast," or shape, the plutonium into pieces. Once cast, the pieces must be fitted together into a whole. Standing near the place where that happens is the first woman to ever assemble pits, whose name we cannot publish for security reasons. She assembled her first pit in 2013 (between 2007 and 2013 the lab produced 31 pits). Today putting a pit together takes her 30 minutes to an hour. "Everything is by touch, by feel," she says. She likes the work, some of which happens in a glove box that's two stories tall. "It's peaceful in the glove box," she says.

Once she or another worker has finished a pit, it gets micromeasured and constitutionally scrutinized to confirm it meets specifications. If it gets a stamp of approval (with a literal stamp, shaped like a diamond), it will go to the Pantex facility in Texas to be placed in a nuclear warhead. In the years to come, if all goes as planned, that process will happen at least 30 times a year here.

All of this effort and investment is being made in the hopes that the pits never serve their active purpose. The U.S., like all nuclear nations, stockpiles weapons in a delicate game of deterrence, the idea being that the existence of our equally or more capable weapons will stop others from using theirs. In this strategy, the pits' true purpose is to sit idly as a threat. But for the strategy to work, the country must be willing to follow through on that threat.

As we leave PF-4, permanently installed instruments once again scan our hands and feet for radiation. After that, in an airlock, a full-body scanner sniffs for alpha, beta and gamma radiation on our bodies. Even though contamination is unlikely, we sigh with relief when the all-clear comes.

We go back to our lives, where we can easily forget about plutonium pits. After the cold war many Americans got used to these weapons. "At some point it became so normal it was forgettable," says Idaho State University nuclear historian Sarah Robey. The fear people feel when confronted with plutonium has degraded over time. But the atomic age is renewing, and we will all have to grapple afresh with the coiled terror of these powerful weapons.

About the Author

Sarah Scoles is a Colorado-based science journalist, a contributing editor at Scientific American *and a senior contributor at Undark. Her newest book is* Countdown: The Blinding Future of Nuclear Weapons *(Bold Type Books, 2024).*

Who Would Take the Brunt of an Attack on U.S. Nuclear Missile Silos?

By Sébastien Philippe

Last March the U.S. Air Force released a two-volume, 3,000-plus-page report detailing the environmental impact of its plans to replace all 400 "Minuteman" land-based intercontinental ballistic missiles (ICBMs) with new "Sentinel" missiles by the mid-2030s. The program is part of a $1.5-trillion effort to modernize the U.S. nuclear arsenal and its command-and-control infrastructure. The report, required by the National Environmental Policy Act of 1970, covers the "potential effects on the human and natural environments from deployment of the Sentinel system" and from, among other things, the refurbishing of existing missile silos and the construction of new utility corridors and communications towers. But it doesn't mention the most significant risks to surrounding communities—namely, what happens if these missiles, which are intended to serve as targets for enemy nuclear weapons, are ever attacked.

The original purpose of the land-based missile system was to deter an enemy nuclear attack by threatening prompt and devastating retaliation, but a key argument for the continued existence—and now the replenishment—of the land-based missiles is to provide a large number of fixed targets meant to exhaust the enemy's resources. Since 1962, when the first ICBMs were installed in the U.S. heartland, competition from other legs of the nuclear triad has forced the rationale for land-based weapons to evolve. By the 1970s, when the U.S. Navy deployed long-range submarine-launched ballistic missiles, the air force had placed 1,000 Minutemen in silos across seven states. As missile-guidance systems improved, it soon became clear that the land-based weapons were vulnerable to attack because of their fixed locations, whereas the stealthy sea-based weapons were much better protected.

The air force used the vulnerability of the land-based missiles to argue for their necessity. In 1978 General Lew Allen, Jr., then air force chief of staff, proposed that the silos offered "a great sponge" of targets in the U.S. to "absorb" incoming Soviet nuclear weapons. Destroying the missile fields would require such a massive attack that adversaries couldn't manage it or even contemplate it. Absent the land-based missiles, the argument goes, an adversary would have far more resources available to seek out and attack other U.S. military and infrastructure targets or even cities.

Even if an adversary is rational enough to not initiate a full-scale attack, the land-based missiles greatly increase the risk of accidental nuclear war. To preclude the possibility of enemy weapons destroying the missiles in their silos, the air force maintains the fleet on high alert, ready to launch on an order from the president–within minutes of enemy missile launches being detected. This "launch on warning" posture makes land-based missiles the most destabilizing leg of the U.S. nuclear triad (which also comprises the missiles based on aerial bombers and submarines). During the cold war there were several false alarms about enemy attacks. If a similar error precipitates the launching of the ICBMs, the adversary will almost certainly retaliate by launching its own nuclear arsenal at military, industrial and demographic targets in the U.S.

Attacking a missile silo requires detonating one or two nuclear warheads, with explosive yields equivalent to 100,000 tons of TNT, close to the buried target. The resulting nuclear explosions will generate gargantuan fireballs that will vaporize everything in their surroundings and produce destructive shock waves capable of wrecking the missiles in their launch tubes. Because the warheads will detonate close to the ground, the nuclear fireballs will suck in soil and other debris and mix it with radioactive bomb effluents as they rise in the air. About 10 minutes after detonation, the mixture of debris and fission products will form miles-high radioactive mushroom clouds, which will then be dispersed by high-altitude winds, leading to fallout on downwind areas.

Studies of the projected fallout from a nuclear attack on the missile fields, published in *Scientific American* in 1976 and 1988, showed that radioactive particles could travel hundreds of miles downwind. A 1990 guide from the Federal Emergency Management Agency on risks and hazards from natural and nuclear calamities confirmed these assessments, adding that no locality in the U.S. was free of the risk of receiving deadly levels of radiation. Today FEMA's publications about the effects of nuclear explosions focus on single nuclear detonations; the agency no longer publishes countrywide assessments of risks from nuclear attacks.

All these past studies relied on relatively simple fallout models and average seasonal winds. Current computational capability, along with higher resolutions in archived weather data, allows scientists to map the radiological risk from a preemptive nuclear attack on the missile silos in unprecedented detail. The results of my simulations, presented here for the first time, paint a harrowing picture of the potential consequences of living with these weapons for the foreseeable future.

According to my models, a concerted nuclear attack on the existing U.S. silo fields—in Colorado, Wyoming, Nebraska, Montana and North Dakota—would annihilate all life in the surrounding regions and contaminate fertile agricultural land for years. Minnesota, Iowa and Kansas would also probably face high levels of radioactive fallout. Acute radiation exposure alone would cause several million fatalities across the U.S.—if people get advance warning and can shelter in place for at least four days. Without appropriate shelter, that number could be twice as high. Because of great variability in wind directions, the entire population of the contiguous U.S. and the most populated areas of Canada, as well as the northern states of Mexico, would be at risk of lethal fallout—more than 300 million people in total. The inhabitants of the U.S. Midwest and of Alberta, Saskatchewan, Manitoba and Ontario in Canada could receive outdoor whole-body doses of radiation several times higher than the minimum known to result in certain death.

Even if there is no nuclear war, people in communities near the missile fields will continue to face serious risks that are also not discussed in the environmental impact statement. One is the accidental release of radioactive materials, such as plutonium, in the warheads by a mechanical shock, fire or explosion. A second is the accidental detonation of a warhead leading to a nuclear explosion. The history of the U.S. nuclear missile program provides several examples of silos or missiles catching fire and of missiles exploding in their launch tubes. One time, in 1964, a warhead fell from the top of its missile to the bottom of its 80-foot-deep silo. Nuclear weapon accidents are not always discussed publicly. The air force hasn't disclosed, for example, the nature of a 2014 "mishap" that occurred while personnel were troubleshooting a Minuteman. The episode caused $1.8 million in damages to the missile, which had to be removed from its silo.

The air force needs to be far more transparent about the true risks of its land-based nuclear missile fleet so the U.S. public can make informed decisions about living with this danger for another half a century.

How Fallout and Fatalities Shift with the Winds

A concerted nuclear attack on the missile silos in the U.S. heartland would generate radioactive dust that travels with prevailing winds. Sébastien Philippe and his colleagues at Princeton University's Program on Science and Global Security used archived weather data to simulate the paths of the resulting plumes for 48 hours, by when most of the dust settles. Because wind directions change daily, the researchers computed fallout dispersal from an 800-kiloton warhead detonating simultaneously at each of 450 silos on any given day of 2021. The scientists further combined these simulations with data on population density and building height to calculate the resulting fatalities. Someone absorbing four grays (equivalent to four joules of radiation energy per kilogram of body weight) would have a 50 percent chance of dying, but people sheltering in bigger buildings would receive smaller doses. Depending on wind directions, a nuclear attack on the missile silos could kill several million people.

Fatality Count: For a simulated attack on any day of 2021, the scientists computed the resulting fatalities. The chart shows the impact of variable wind directions on the estimated fatalities after four days of exposure. The estimates range from 340,000 (for an attack on July 1) to 4.6 million (on December 2). The average estimated death toll is 1.4 million. The curve shows the probability

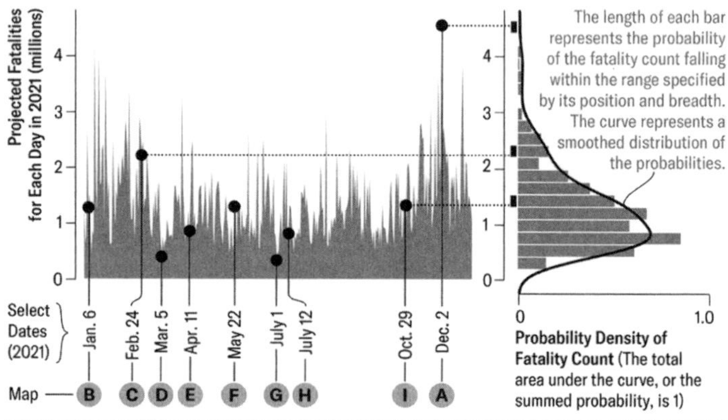

Credit: Sébastien Philippe, Svitlana Lavrenchuk and Ivan Stepanov

(technically, probability density) of the number of fatalities specified on the vertical axis.

Which Locations Are the Riskiest?

To calculate the average risk of radiation exposure at any given location in North America from a nuclear attack on the silo fields, Philippe and his co-workers summed the simulated outcomes for any day of 2021 and divided by 365. They thereby averaged the impact of shifting winds on radioactive fallout across the continent. This map shows the average outdoor radiation dose across North America after four days of exposure. Communities living closest to the silos could receive several times more than 8 Gy, which scientists regard as lethal. Most inhabitants of Montana, North Dakota, South Dakota, Nebraska and Minnesota would get average doses greater than 1 Gy, causing fatalities from acute radiation syndrome, especially among children. The U.S. population would receive average doses greater than 0.001 Gy per year, which is the current annual limit for exposure to the public.

The Worst-Case Scenarios

Sifting through simulations for each day of 2021, the Princeton researchers computed the worst possible outcome at each location

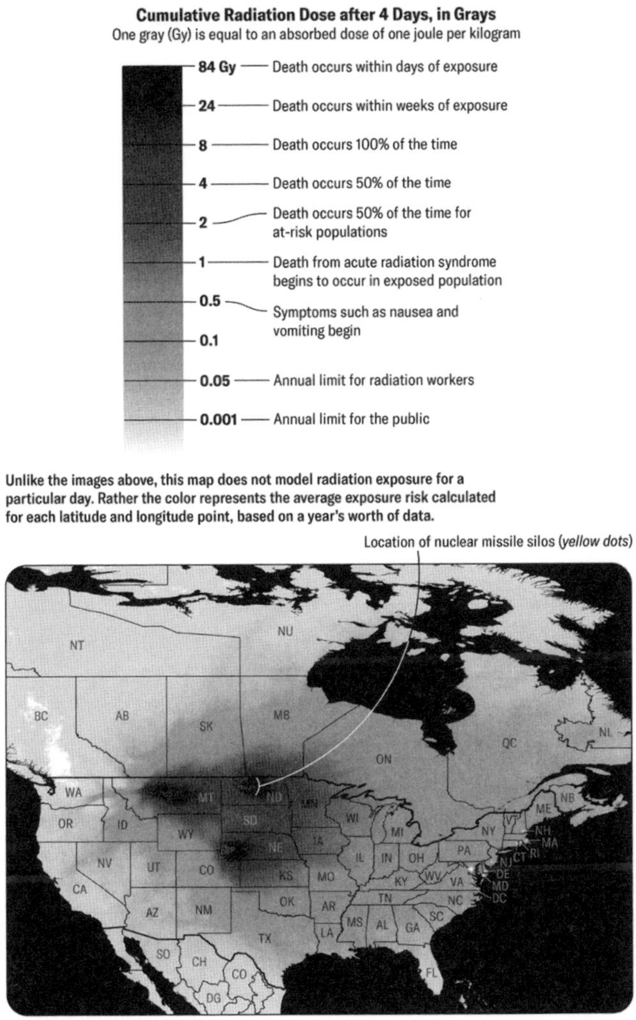

Credit: Sébastien Philippe, Svitlana Lavrenchuk and Ivan Stepanov

from a concerted nuclear attack on the missile silos. This map shows all the worst-case scenarios across North America. Not all locations would experience the worst outcome from the same attack; which areas would be impacted depends on wind patterns on the day of the attack. Overall, most people in North America live in areas with about a 1 percent chance of receiving an outdoor dose greater than 1 Gy. The chance of getting a lethal dose escalates closer to the silos, with three million at risk of receiving 8 Gy or more. These simulations make no assumptions about access to health care or

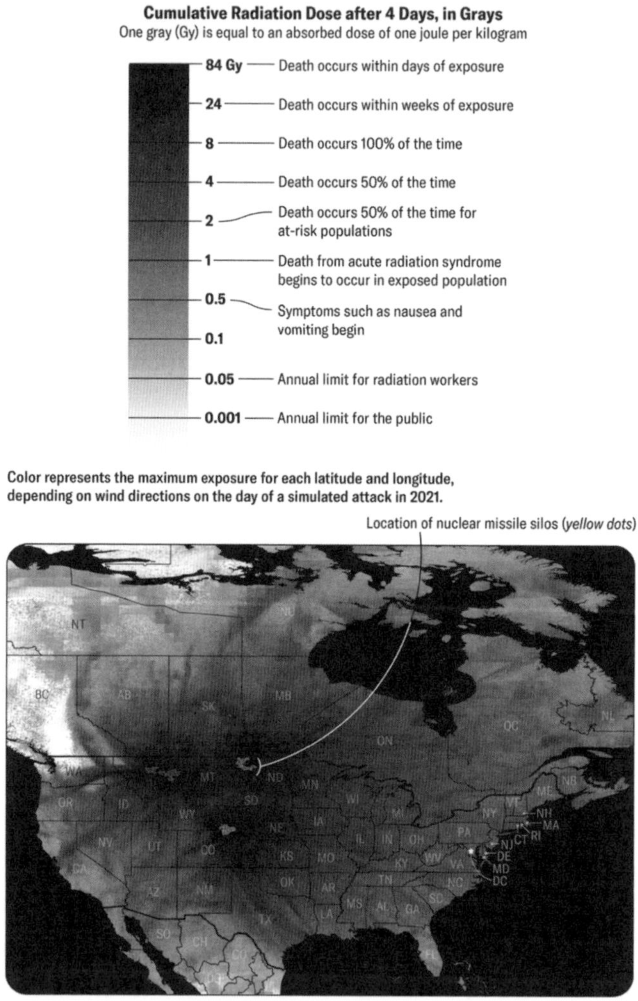

Credit: Sébastien Philippe, Svitlana Lavrenchuk and Ivan Stepanov

emergency services. Nor do they include other sources of exposure such as immediate radiation from nuclear explosions.

About the Author

Sébastien Philippe is a scientist at Princeton University's Program on Science and Global Security. He develops methods for monitoring nuclear weapons and models the impact of nuclear explosions..

Section 7: Quirks of Nuclear Physics

The Workings of an Ancient Nuclear Reactor

By Alex P. Meshik

In May 1972 a worker at a nuclear fuel-processing plant in France noticed something suspicious. He had been conducting a routine analysis of uranium derived from a seemingly ordinary source of ore. As is the case with all natural uranium, the material under study contained three isotopes—that is to say, three forms with differing atomic masses: uranium 238, the most abundant variety; uranium 234, the rarest; and uranium 235, the isotope that is coveted because it can sustain a nuclear chain reaction. Elsewhere in the earth's crust, on the moon and even in meteorites, uranium 235 atoms make up 0.720 percent of the total. But in these samples, which came from the Oklo deposit in Gabon (a former French colony in west equatorial Africa), uranium 235 constituted just 0.717 percent. That tiny discrepancy was enough to alert French scientists that something strange had happened. Further analyses showed that ore from at least one part of the mine was far short on uranium 235: some 200 kilograms appeared to be missing—enough to make half a dozen or so nuclear bombs.

For weeks, specialists at the French Atomic Energy Commission (CEA) remained perplexed. The answer came only when someone recalled a prediction published 19 years earlier. In 1953 George W. Wetherill of the University of California at Los Angeles and Mark G. Inghram of the University of Chicago pointed out that some uranium deposits might have once operated as natural versions of the nuclear fission reactors that were then becoming popular. Shortly thereafter, Paul K. Kuroda, a chemist from the University of Arkansas, calculated what it would take for a uranium-ore body spontaneously to undergo self-sustained fission. In this process, a stray neutron causes a uranium 235 nucleus to split, which gives off more neutrons, causing others of these atoms to break apart in a nuclear chain reaction.

Kuroda's first condition was that the size of the uranium deposit should exceed the average length that fission-inducing neutrons travel, about two thirds of a meter. This requirement helps to ensure that the neutrons given off by one fissioning nucleus are absorbed by another before escaping from the uranium vein.

A second prerequisite is that uranium 235 must be present in sufficient abundance. Today even the most massive and concentrated uranium deposit cannot become a nuclear reactor, because the uranium 235 concentration, at less than 1 percent, is just too low. But this isotope is radioactive and decays about six times faster than does uranium 238, which indicates that the fissile fraction was much higher in the distant past. For example, two billion years ago (about when the Oklo deposit formed) uranium 235 must have constituted approximately 3 percent, which is roughly the level provided artificially in the enriched uranium used to fuel most nuclear power stations.

The third important ingredient is a neutron "moderator," a substance that can slow the neutrons given off when a uranium nucleus splits so that they are more apt to induce other uranium nuclei to break apart. Finally, there should be no significant amounts of boron, lithium or other so-called poisons, which absorb neutrons and would thus bring any nuclear reaction to a swift halt.

Amazingly, the actual conditions that prevailed two billion years ago in what researchers eventually determined to be 16 separate areas within the Oklo and adjacent Okelobondo uranium mines were very close to what Kuroda outlined. These zones were all identified decades ago. But only recently did my colleagues and I finally clarify major details of what exactly went on inside one of those ancient reactors.

Proof in the Light Elements

Physicists confirmed the basic idea that natural fission reactions were responsible for the depletion in uranium 235 at Oklo quite soon after the anomalous uranium was discovered. Indisputable proof came from an examination of the new, lighter elements created when a heavy nucleus is broken in two. The abundance of these fission products proved so high that no other conclusion could be drawn. A nuclear chain reaction very much like the one that Enrico Fermi and his colleagues famously demonstrated in 1942 had certainly taken place, all on its own and some two billion years before.

Shortly after this astonishing discovery, physicists from around the world studied the evidence for these natural nuclear reactors and came together to share their work on "the Oklo phenomenon" at a special 1975 conference held in Libreville, the capital of Gabon. The next year George A. Cowan, who represented the U.S. at that meeting (and who, incidentally, is one of the founders of the renowned Santa Fe Institute, where he is still affiliated), wrote an article for *Scientific American* in which he explained what scientists had surmised about the operation of these ancient reactors.

Cowan described, for example, how some of the neutrons released during the fission of uranium 235 were captured by the more abundant uranium 238, which became uranium 239 and, after emitting two electrons, turned into plutonium 239. More than two tons of this plutonium isotope were generated within the Oklo deposit. Although almost all this material, which has a 24,000-year halflife, has since disappeared (primarily through natural radioactive decay), some of the plutonium itself underwent fission, as attested by the presence of its characteristic fission products. The abundance of those lighter elements allowed scientists to deduce that fission reactions must have gone on for hundreds of thousands of years. From the amount of uranium 235 consumed, they calculated the total energy released, 15,000 megawatt-years, and from this and other evidence were able to work out the average power output, which was probably less than 100 kilowatts–say, enough to run a few dozen toasters.

It is truly amazing that more than a dozen natural reactors spontaneously sprang into existence and that they managed to maintain a modest power output for perhaps a few hundred millennia. Why is it that these parts of the deposit did not explode and destroy themselves right after nuclear chain reactions began? What mechanism provided the necessary self-regulation? Did these reactors run steadily or in fits and starts? The solutions to these puzzles emerged slowly after initial discovery of the Oklo phenomenon. Indeed, the last question lingered for more than three decades before my colleagues and I at Washington University in St. Louis began to address it by examining a piece of this enigmatic African ore.

Noble-Gas Epiphanies

Our recent work on one of the Oklo reactors centered on an analysis of xenon, a heavy inert gas, which can remain imprisoned within minerals for billions of years. Xenon possesses nine stable isotopes, produced in various proportions by different nuclear processes. Being a noble gas, it resists chemical bonding with other elements and is thus easy to purify for isotopic analysis. Xenon is extremely rare, which allows scientists to use it to detect and trace nuclear reactions, even those that occurred in primitive meteorites before the solar system came into existence.

To analyze the isotopic composition of xenon requires a mass spectrometer, an instrument that can separate atoms according to their atomic weight. I was fortunate to have access to an extremely accurate xenon mass spectrometer, one built by my Washington colleague Charles M. Hohenberg. But before using his apparatus, we had to extract the xenon from our sample. Scientists usually just heat the host material, often above the melting point, so that the rock loses its crystalline structure and cannot hold on to its hidden cache of xenon. To glean greater information about the genesis and retention of this gas, we adopted a more delicate approach called laser extraction, which releases xenon selectively from a single mineral grain, leaving adjacent areas intact.

We applied this technique to many tiny spots on our lone available fragment of Oklo rock, only one millimeter thick and four millimeters across. Of course, we first needed to decide where exactly to aim the laser beam. Here Hohenberg and I relied on our colleague Olga Pravdivtseva, who had constructed a detailed x-ray map of our sample and identified the constituent minerals. After each extraction, we purified the resulting gas and passed the xenon into Hohenberg's mass spectrometer, which indicated the number of atoms of each isotope present.

Our first surprise was the location of the xenon. It was not, as we had expected, found to a significant extent in the uranium-rich mineral grains. Rather the lion's share was trapped in aluminum phosphate minerals, which contain no uranium at all. Remarkably, these grains showed the highest concentration of xenon ever found in any natural material. The second epiphany was that the extracted gas had a significantly different isotopic makeup from what is usually produced in nuclear reactors. It had seemingly lost a large portion of the xenon 136 and 134 that would certainly have been created from fission, whereas the lighter varieties of the element were modified to a lesser extent.

How could such a change in isotopic composition have come about? Chemical reactions would not do the trick, because all isotopes are chemically identical. Perhaps nuclear reactions, such as neutron capture? Careful analysis allowed my colleagues and me to reject this possibility as well. We also considered the physical sorting of different isotopes that sometimes takes place: heavier atoms move a bit more slowly than their lighter counterparts and can thus sometimes separate from them. Uranium enrichment plants—industrial facilities that require considerable skill to construct—take advantage of this property to produce reactor fuel. But even if nature could miraculously create a similar process on a microscopic scale, the mix of xenon isotopes in the aluminum phosphate grains we studied would have been different from what we found. For example, measured with respect to the amount of xenon 132 present, the depletion of xenon 136 (being four atomic mass units heavier) would have been twice that of xenon 134 (two atomic mass units heavier) if physical sorting had operated. We did not see that pattern.

Our understanding of the anomalous composition of the xenon came only after we thought harder about how this gas was born. None of the xenon isotopes we measured were the direct result of uranium fission. Rather they were the products of the decay of radioactive isotopes of iodine, which in turn were formed from radioactive tellurium and so forth, according to a well-known sequence of nuclear reactions that gives rise to stable xenon.

Our key insight was the realization that different xenon isotopes in our Oklo sample were created at different times—following a schedule that depended on the half-lives of their iodine parents and tellurium grandparents. The longer a particular radioactive precursor lives, the longer xenon formation from it is held off. For example, production of xenon 136 began at Oklo only about a minute after the onset of self-sustained fission. An hour later the next lighter stable isotope, xenon 134, appeared. Then, some days after the start of fission, xenon 132 and 131 came on the scene. Finally, after millions of years, and well after the nuclear chain reactions terminated, xenon 129 formed.

Had the Oklo deposit remained a closed system, the xenon accumulated during operation of its natural reactors would have preserved the normal isotopic composition produced by fission. But scientists have no reason to think that the system was closed. Indeed, there is good cause to suspect the opposite. The evidence comes from a consideration of the simple fact that the Oklo reactors somehow regulated themselves. The most likely mechanism involves the action of groundwater, which presumably boiled away after the temperature reached some critical level. Without water present to act as a neutron moderator, nuclear chain reactions would have temporarily ceased. Only after things cooled off and sufficient groundwater once again permeated the zone of reaction could fission resume.

This picture of how the Oklo reactors probably worked highlights two important points: very likely they pulsed on and off in some fashion, and large quantities of water must have been moving through these rocks—enough to wash away some of the xenon precursors, tellurium and iodine, which are water-soluble. The presence of water also helps to explain why most of the xenon now resides in grains of aluminum phosphate rather than in the uranium rich minerals where fission first created these radioactive precursors. The xenon did not simply migrate from one set of preexisting minerals to another—it is unlikely that aluminum phosphate minerals were present before the

Oklo reactors began operating. Instead those grains of aluminum phosphate probably formed in place through the action of the nuclear-heated water, once it had cooled to about 300 degrees Celsius.

During each active period of operation of an Oklo reactor and for some time afterward, while the temperature remained high, much of the xenon gas (including xenon 136 and 134, which were generated relatively quickly) was driven off. When the reactor cooled down, the longer-lived xenon precursors (those that would later spawn xenon 132, 131 and 129, which we found in relative abundance) were preferentially incorporated into growing grains of aluminum phosphate. Then, as more water returned to the reaction zone, neutrons became properly moderated and fission once again resumed, allowing the cycle of heating and cooling to repeat. The result was the peculiar segregation of xenon isotopes we uncovered.

It is not entirely obvious what forces kept this xenon inside the aluminum phosphate minerals for almost half the planet's lifetime. In particular, why was the xenon generated during a given operational pulse not driven off during the next one? Presumably it became imprisoned in the cagelike structure of the aluminum phosphate minerals, which were able to hold on to the xenon gas created within them, even at high temperatures. The details remain fuzzy, but whatever the final answers are, one thing is clear: the capacity of aluminum phosphate for capturing xenon is truly amazing.

Nature's Operating Schedule

After my colleagues and I had worked out in a general way how the observed set of xenon isotopes was created inside the aluminum phosphate grains, we attempted to model the process mathematically. This exercise revealed much about the timing of reactor operation, with all xenon isotopes providing pretty much the same answer. The Oklo reactor we studied had switched "on" for 30 minutes and "off" for at least 2.5 hours. The pattern is not unlike what one sees in some geysers, which slowly heat up, boil off their supply of groundwater in a spectacular display, refill, and repeat the cycle, day in and day out, year after year. This similarity supports the notion not only that groundwater passing through the Oklo deposit was a neutron moderator but also that its boiling away at times accounted for the self-regulation that protected these natural reactors from destruction. In this regard, it was extremely effective, allowing not a single meltdown or explosion during hundreds of thousands of years.

One would imagine that engineers working in the nuclear power industry could learn a thing or two from Oklo. And they certainly can, though not necessarily about reactor design. The more important lessons may be about how to handle nuclear waste. Oklo, after all, serves as a good analogue for a long-term geologic repository, which is why scientists have examined in great detail how the various products of fission have migrated away from these natural reactors over time. They have also scrutinized a similar zone of ancient nuclear fission found in exploratory boreholes drilled at a site called Bangombe, located some 35 kilometers away. The Bangombe reactor is of special interest because it was more shallowly buried than those unearthed at the Oklo and Okelobondo mines and thus has had more water moving through it in recent times. In all, the observations boost confidence that many kinds of dangerous nuclear waste can be successfully sequestered underground.

Oklo also demonstrates a way to store some forms of nuclear waste that were once thought to be almost impossible to prevent from contaminating the environment. Since the advent of nuclear power generation, huge amounts of radioactive xenon 135, krypton 85 and other inert gases that nuclear plants generate have been released into the atmosphere. Nature's fission reactors suggest the possibility of locking those waste products away in aluminum phosphate minerals, which have a unique ability to capture and retain such gases for billions of years.

The Oklo reactors may also teach scientists about possible shifts in what was formerly thought to be a fundamental physical constant, one called α (alpha), which controls such universal quantities as the speed of light [see "Inconstant Constants," by John D. Barrow and John K. Webb; *Scientific American*]. For three decades, the two-billion-year old

Oklo phenomenon has been used to argue against α having changed. But last year Steven K. Lamoreaux and Justin R. Torgerson of Los Alamos National Laboratory drew on Oklo to posit that this "constant" has, in fact, varied significantly (and, strangely enough, in the opposite sense from what others have recently proposed). Lamoreaux and Torgerson's calculations hinge on certain details about how Oklo operated, and in that respect the work my colleagues and I have done might help elucidate this perplexing issue.

Were these ancient reactors in Gabon the only ones ever to have formed on the earth? Two billion years ago the conditions necessary for self-sustained fission must not have been too rare, so perhaps other natural reactors will one day be discovered. I expect that a few telltale wisps of xenon could aid immensely in this search.

NASA's 'Nuclear Option' May Be Crucial for Getting Humans to Mars

By David W. Brown; edited by Lee Billings

The pathway to humans on Mars lies through the atom, split.

Far from Earth, whether in the void or on another world, power is life. A steady, strong flow of electricity is as crucial for operating computers and engines as it is for assuring access to corporeal necessities such as light and heat, breathable air and potable water, and preparation or even growth of food. And one of the most potent and reliable ways to get all those vital kilowatts is via nuclear fission—something aspiring astronauts realized long before anyone ever reached space (or developed nuclear weapons, for that matter). Yet more than 60 years into the space age, nuclear fission for spaceflight remains mostly a dream. Now, however, as NASA pursues its Apollo-esque Artemis program to build a crewed lunar outpost (with an eye toward eventual human landings on Mars), a rare alignment of technology, funding and political will is on the verge of making spaceborne nuclear reactors a routine reality.

In 2020 the White House gave NASA a 10-year deadline to deliver a 10-kilowatt nuclear power system to the surface of the moon. The project is now a top priority of the agency's Space Technology Mission Directorate. And in July 2021 congressional appropriators earmarked $110 million for NASA to advance development of a new nuclear rocket suitable for sending cargo and crew on interplanetary voyages. NASA had not even asked for the money.

The reason for this sudden urgency is simple: Without nuclear power, the space agency's stated goal of establishing a moon base by the end of the decade—let alone putting boots on Mars—becomes difficult, if not impossible, to achieve.

Surprisingly, no fundamental technology breakthroughs are required to build a nuclear reactor for spaceflight applications. (In fact, the U.S. already did so once—and so far only once—with the Air Force's development and launch of a working prototype in 1965.) Instead the difficulty lies in navigating the complex web of regulations that surrounds all things nuclear and in ensuring any chosen approach for nuclear power beyond Earth does not needlessly limit NASA to just the lunar surface or any other lone deep-space destination. Ideally, the power of the atom can be harnessed not only for crewed missions to the moon and Mars but also for robotic exploration throughout the solar system.

"The goal going in is make sure that what we use on the moon from a fission reactor standpoint is also directly applicable for use on the surface of Mars," says Michael Houts, manager of nuclear research at NASA's Marshall Space Flight Center.

Fission, he explains, is a pretty simple process. "It's literally just the right materials in the right geometry," Houts says. "That's why, once it was discovered, we very quickly had systems able to self-sustain a chain reaction." This differs completely from the radioisotope thermoelectric generators (RTGs) that power NASA's Mars rovers, the New Horizons mission to Pluto and beyond, and the *Voyager* spacecraft now in interstellar space. RTGs merely convert the heat released from naturally decaying plutonium into electricity. Fission reactors are far more powerful and versatile, splitting atoms from uranium fuel and channeling the released energy into propulsion and electricity production.

"There are no physics breakthroughs needed, no miracles necessary. But just like terrestrial systems, you're going to need to have some really good engineering," Houts says.

A Long-Delayed Giant Leap

NASA is publicly cagey about its Mars timeline, but since the first term of former president George W. Bush, the agency has steadily worked toward a giant leap on the Martian surface by the end of the 2030s. In 2020 NASA asked the National Academies of Sciences, Engineering, and Medicine to study the technical challenges, benefits and risks of nuclear propulsion, with particular emphasis on a notional nuclear-propelled cargo launch to Mars in 2033 that would precede a human mission in 2039.

In logistic terms, what such a mission would look like has scarcely changed since the 1950s. Three years before Yuri Gagarin's flight made humans a spacefaring species, NASA's precursor, the National Advisory Committee for Aeronautics, began a formal study of nuclear propulsion as part of a crewed Mars expedition. This investigation called for a 420-day expedition with 40 days at Mars. Other, more ambitious proposals have examined lengthier surface sojourns on Mars stretching to around 500 days, but the classic mission profile has remained the dominant vision for crewed Mars exploration, driven in part by celestial mechanics and reasons of survival: To conserve fuel, both Earth and Mars must be properly aligned in their orbit. And technologically speaking, humans are not yet ready to cut the terrestrial umbilical cord and truly "live off the land" in space.

The human body can handle the journey, as evidenced by decades of data from crews living and working on space stations in low-Earth orbit. The current record for the longest continuous stay in space is held by the cosmonaut Valeri Polyakov. Thanks to a vigorous off-world workout regimen, he was able to walk from his capsule after landing despite having spent 437 days in muscle-wasting microgravity onboard the Soviet space station Mir. Upon returning to Earth, Polyakov's first words to a fellow cosmonaut reportedly were "We can fly to Mars."

NASA's current goal for a Mars mission calls for a round trip of about two years. Nuclear propulsion would be a critical enabler. In addition to increasing the number of flight opportunities for a crewed mission, it would reduce the number of flights necessary to get the fuel for such a trip into Earth's orbit.

Those fuel requirements are considerable. The International Space Station, painstakingly built via more than three dozen launches across a decade's time, is approximately 420 metric tons. A chemical propulsion system necessary for a round trip to Mars would require the very expensive task of lofting somewhere between more than twice to nearly 10 times as much tonnage from Earth.

Consider that the mightiest of NASA's rockets–the Space Launch System (SLS), which has yet to even fly–is slated to carry a mere 95 metric tons to space at $2 billion per launch. If–or when–the SLS is superseded by more capable and cost-effective rockets such as SpaceX's in-development and all-reusable Starship, that single-launch mass limit will increase to more than 100 metric tons, and the price per launch should plummet. Even so, the financial calculus of a chemically fueled Mars mission would still be daunting.

In contrast, an analogous Mars mission using nuclear propulsion would require sending up a total mass of between 500 and 1,000 metric tons. Launching the equivalent of a single space station–maybe two–is plausible. After all, we have done it before.

Hard Choices

NASA is presently pursuing not one but two classes of atomic-powered rocketry: nuclear thermal propulsion and nuclear electric propulsion. Either of these approaches could pair with nuclear surface power–the third key fission technology under study by the space agency.

Nuclear thermal propulsion implemented on the interplanetary scale would essentially be a ferry or transfer stage–a smaller nuclear-powered rocket that would dock with other transport elements in orbit before pushing its separately launched payload onward. Such an arrangement operates much like a chemical propulsion system, although the combustion chamber–where a rocket's fuel and oxidizer mix and ignite, producing hot exhaust forced from the rocket nozzle–is replaced with a nuclear reactor that heats a cryogenic propellant, blasting it through the nozzle to generate thrust. The process, viewed externally, looks virtually identical: a rocket engine blasting fire.

Nuclear electric propulsion, on the other hand, works a lot like a nuclear power plant on Earth, in which fission reactions are used (via an intermediate step such as driving a turbine) to generate electricity. That electricity, in turn, can power an electric propulsion system similar to (but far stronger than) the solar-powered ion thrusters on NASA's *Dawn*, a spacecraft that explored the asteroid Vesta and dwarf planet Ceres.

There are trade-offs to each approach. The greatest challenge of nuclear thermal propulsion is that it is a high-performance reactor operating at a high temperature, reaching circa 2,500 degrees Celsius– an unnerving prospect for astronauts and materials engineers. The reactor would also require immense volumes of cryogenic propellant, likely sourced from on-orbit storage tanks that carry major engineering challenges of their own. But the approach's focused intensity has an upside: "The propulsion system only needs to run for a few hours total," Houts says. "You get all your [work] done very quickly." After that, the spacecraft has all the speed it needs for a trip to Mars or home.

Nuclear electric propulsion, meanwhile, runs at lower temperatures and power levels, but it must operate continuously for months or even years, building fantastic speeds over time. It is a more complex system than its thermal counterpart in many ways. And it is less developed: the calculated performance levels for near-term designs are far below what would be necessary for a crewed mission to Mars. The power produced by a nuclear electric propulsion system's reactor must be converted multiple times (rather than just being absorbed and dissipated by propellant blown out the back of a rocket). Conversions can only be done with efficiency percentages ranging from the mid-30s to 40.The rest of that thermal energy must somehow be dealt with: present concepts call for massive radiators to dissipate the excess heat into space. The nuclear electric spacecraft would also require a short, sharp kick from an old-fashioned chemical propulsion system to help it escape Earth's orbit and another to enter and depart orbit around Mars.

Past and Future

In part because of its relative simplicity, nuclear thermal propulsion is the clear favorite among Mars mission planners–and U.S. politicians. This was the approach that netted the $110-million endorsement of congressional appropriators in July 2021 and that the NASA-sponsored National Academies report flagged as most plausible for enabling a 2039 crewed mission to the Red Planet.

Nuclear thermal propulsion also has the advantage of a rich inheritance: The U.S. government–chiefly the Department of Defense–has been fitfully trying to get the technology flying since the dawn of the space age. One bold early attempt traces to a 1955 Air Force effort known as Project Rover, which sought to build a nuclear thermal upper stage for intercontinental ballistic missiles. But chemical propulsion soon proved sufficient for that job, so Rover was absorbed into NASA, where it became the Nuclear Engine for Rocket Vehicle Application (NERVA) program. In the late 1950s, the DoD started work on the Systems for Nuclear Auxiliary Power (SNAP) program, an effort to launch space nuclear reactors to power long-duration missions such as spy satellites.

Both projects achieved impressive results. SNAP led to the Air Force's 1965 launch of SNAP-10A, the only U.S. fission reactor ever sent to space. The reactor functioned for six weeks in orbit. NERVA, meanwhile, successfully developed and tested nuclear thermal rockets on Earth. And the program was, for a time, central to NASA's post-Apollo plans for Mars exploration. But the Nixon administration instead chose to pursue the space shuttle and canceled both projects in 1973. NERVA was briefly resurrected in the late 1980s by an Air Force–led effort, the Space Nuclear Thermal Propulsion program, but by the early 1990s interest had fizzled again.

Nuclear electric propulsion, too, had its brief moment in NASA's limelight. In 2003 an initiative called Project Prometheus brought together NASA, the U.S. Navy's submarine reactor program and the Department of Energy–this time to build a nuclear electric propulsion fleet for science missions. Spaceborne fission would enable a single spacecraft to explore multiple targets in the outer solar system and even beyond, where sparse sunlight profoundly limits solar power's potential. Project Prometheus would have been nothing short of revolutionary: its reactor would have produced 200,000 watts of power for a spacecraft's propulsion and instruments. (By comparison, the *New Horizons* probe operates on just 200 watts of power–that is, about two or three incandescent light bulbs' worth.) NASA,however, snuffed out Prometheus after two years, citing budget concerns.

One might think all these past projects would be a huge boost for today's push to develop atomic-powered rocketry, but their mercurial nature makes them of limited use.

"Historically, if you spend three or four years developing a nuclear propulsion system, and then you stop, and you come back a decade later, you've got to recapture a lot of knowledge," says Shannon Bragg-Sitton, a leading nuclear engineer at the Idaho National Laboratory and co-author of the National Academies report. "The fact that we've been looking at both these systems since the 1950s doesn't mean that we have 70 years of knowledge. It means that we started thinking about them then, and we made some efforts in each of them."

NASA's notional target date of 2039 for a crewed Mars mission might seem so far off that urgent action is not yet necessary, but Bragg-Sitton says the timing is deceptive. The tentative plan calls for nuclear-powered cargo flights to begin six years earlier, in 2033, to preposition materials on Mars and serve as dry runs for crewed transport. "We need to be ready to actually launch our first system for qualification with those supply missions," she says. "Well, now the timeline is not as long as it sounded initially!" Ideally, she says, hardware designs for a flight in 2033 would be locked-in by 2027. That means the time is now to make critical decisions, chief among them comparing and choosing between nuclear thermal and nuclear electric propulsion.

"You can't develop a nuclear system in a year or two–it's just the way it is," Bragg-Sitton concludes. "None of this is out of our reach. It just takes a lot of focus to get it done."

But first, someone needs to let them do it.

The DRACO Wager

Getting approval to launch nuclear materials into space, it turns out, is at least as challenging as actually building a space-ready nuclear reactor or rocket. This is especially true if your fission system relies on highly enriched uranium—that is, uranium composed of 20 percent or more of the fissile isotope uranium 235. Only 1 percent of Earth's naturally occurring uranium takes this form, which is prized by warhead designers and spacecraft engineers striving to make their creations as featherweight and powerful as possible. The more uranium 235 your nuclear fuel has, the smaller you can make your reactor—or your bomb, which is why the material is subject to such strict regulations.

For NASA, even a nuclear payload without highly enriched uranium has enormous hurdles to clear—namely a labyrinthine safety analysis process that often involves many other federal agencies and culminates in NASA's administrator approving or rejecting a launch. If a rocket carries highly enriched uranium, however, it can only be launched after formal authorization from the White House. The additional stringency associated with this highest tier of approval can easily add several years and tens of millions of dollars to a project's schedule and budget.

Find a way to avoid using highly enriched uranium, then, and you may secure a far faster and cheaper path to the launchpad. There are, in fact, new designs for advanced high-power reactors that use large amounts of low-enriched uranium rather than small amounts of highly enriched material. But whether or not NASA ultimately pursues such an approach for its nuclear aspirations may be dictated by the work of another federal entity: the Defense Advanced Research Projects Agency wants to launch one of these new reactors to space by 2025 to power a proof-of-concept nuclear propulsion system—a timeline that would be aggressive even by Apollo standards. DARPA calls the system the Demonstration Rocket for Agile Cislunar Operations, or DRACO. The program's murky origins involve DoD demands for some of its classified missions to have the capability to maneuver in space faster than would be possible through chemical propulsion.

DARPA's gamble with DRACO is twofold: it seeks to reach the launchpad quickly by using a new type of reactor and by minimizing Earth-based trials, thus bypassing the presidential-tier launch approval process and a rat's nest of ground-testing red tape. This bold strategy arose from the agency's judgment that such tests are now virtually impossible to perform because of prohibitive regulations and inadequate infrastructure. One cannot, for instance, simply update and use the specialized facilities that supported NERVA testing–they were razed when the program ended. Building new test facilities is undesirable, too, because doing so would require billions of dollars and several years of work during which the project could easily be scuttled by shifting political priorities. Although DARPA's accelerated plan calls for robust ground testing of DRACO's smaller components, this does not include operating the full reactor at full power. Astoundingly, the very first time DRACO's reactor would turn on would be in space.

"Starting the reactor is going to be entirely based on our predictions," says Tabitha Dodson, a project manager for DRACO at DARPA. "We are going to put a lot of guesswork into our modeling and simulations before launching the engine, without ever having tested it on the ground." Data from the NERVA tests of yore should help, Dodson says, but the task before the DRACO team remains "extremely challenging."

After more than a half-century of starts and stops, says Air Force major Nathan Greiner, another DARPA project manager, launching a nuclear reactor would be a critical enabler. "Let's get this all the way across the finish line–not just small elements, not just a reactor on the ground, but, no kidding, let's go build a spacecraft and put it in space," he says. Such an "existence proof" would then ease the way for NASA or the DoD in any future overtures to congressional appropriators. The question would no longer be "Does this technology exist?" but rather "Do you want more of it–or not?"

Let's Get Serious

Of course, DARPA alone cannot spark a spaceflight revolution. Nuclear propulsion for space exploration is a whole-of-government effort. At minimum, the Department of Energy will need to make more low-enriched uranium. One agency or another–most likely, several working together–will have to develop orbital fuel depots to provide outbound missions with cryogenic propellants and will have to find better, safer ways to perform ground tests of interplanetary-scale propulsion systems. And then NASA must actually build the rockets.

DRACO will not get NASA and its astronauts all the way to Mars, Greiner says, "but this is going to take it a hell of a long way along that path."

If nothing else, today's push for nuclear power in space is a useful metric for measuring the seriousness of NASA's—and the nation's—lunar and Martian ambitions. In the context of human spaceflight, NASA has a well-known aversion to "new" (and thus presumably more risky) technology—but in this case, the "old" way makes an already perilous human endeavor needlessly difficult. For all the challenges of embracing nuclear power for pushing the horizon outward for humans in space, it is hard to make the case that tried-and-true chemical propulsion is easier or carries significantly less physical—and political—risk. Launching 10 International Space Stations' worth of mass across 27 superheavy rocket launches for fuel alone for a single Mars mission would be a difficult pace for NASA to sustain. (That is more than 40 launches and at least $80 billion if the agency relies on the SLS.) And such a scenario assumes everything goes perfectly: sending help to a troubled crew on or around Mars would require dozens of additional fuel launches, and chemical propulsion allows very limited windows of opportunity for the liftoff of any rescue mission.

If, with a single technology, that alarmingly high number of ludicrously expensive launches could be cut down to three—while also offering more chances to travel to Mars and back—how could a space agency that was earnest in its ambitions not pursue that approach? No miracles are necessary, and regulators and appropriators seem to agree that the time has come.

As Polyakov said, "We can fly to Mars." Splitting atoms, it seems, is now the safest way to make that happen.

About the Author

David W. Brown a writer based in New Orleans. His next book, The Outside Cats, *will be published by Mariner Books. Follow him on Twitter.*

GLOSSARY

arsenal A collection of weaponry held for possible conflict.

entrepreneur An individual who creates a business.

fission A nuclear reaction characterized by the splitting of an atom, with a resulting release of energy.

fuel rod A manufactured metal tube containing nuclear fuel, used in nuclear power plants.

fusion A nuclear reaction characterized by the joining of atoms together, with a resulting release of energy.

heavy water A molecule to water, but with its hydrogen atom replaced with deuterium, a hydrogen isotope. Heavy water is used in some nuclear reactions.

impasse A point of impossibility or necessary decision-making.

isotope A specific type of a chemical element. Isotopoes of the same element can have different numbers of neutrons, and have different properties.

kilowatt hour A unit for measuring the energy capacity of a power plant.

light-water reactor A power plant that uses ordinary water instead of heavy water.

modular Able to be combined into larger units.

neutron Particle at the center of an atom, with no positive or negative charge.

nucleus The center of the atom, comprised of protons and neutrons. Fusion or fission reactions take place in the nucleus and give "nuclear" its name.

ore The form metal takes when it is mined from the earth, mixed with other substances that must be removed.

panacea A term originating in medicine meaning a cure for anything. Panacea is also used to imply a tool that can solve any problem.

plutonium A heavy element used in nuclear reactions, typically in human-made forms due to its rarity.

preclude To prevent or hinder.

proton Particle at the center of an atom, with a positive charge.

radiation Energy emitted from matter.

radioactive In a state of emitting radiation.

radioactive decay The slow disappearance of a radioactive substance over time.

reactor A facility that produces energy.

repository Place designated for the storage and protection of something.

spall To break off chips, scales, or slabs.

uranium A naturally-occurring heavy element used in nuclear reactions.

warhead The explosive device at the tip of a missile or other weapon.

FURTHER INFORMATION

American Nuclear Society. "Nuclear Science 101." *American Nuclear Society*, https://www.ans.org/nuclear/science/.

Ball, Philip. "U.S. Project Reaches Major Milestone toward Practical Fusion Power." *Scientific American*, February 2, 2022, https://www.scientificamerican.com/article/u-s-project-reaches-major-milestone-toward-practical-fusion-power/.

Bartels, Meghan. "Turtle Shells Record Nuclear History." *Scientific American*, August 22, 2023, https://www.scientificamerican.com/article/turtle-shells-record-nuclear-history/.

Galindo, Andrea. "What is Nuclear Energy? The Science of Nuclear Power." *International Atomic Energy Agency*, November 15, 2022, https://www.iaea.org/newscenter/news/what-is-nuclear-energy-the-science-of-nuclear-power.

Hughes-Castleberry, Kenna. "New Results Reveal How to Build a Nuclear Clock." *Scientific American*, November 1, 2023, https://www.scientificamerican.com/article/new-results-reveal-how-to-build-a-nuclear-clock/.

Kristensen, et al. "Status of World Nuclear Forces." *Federation of American Scientists*, March 29, 2024, https://fas.org/initiative/status-world-nuclear-forces/.

Kuperman, Alan J. "U.S. Plan to Put Weapons-Grade Uranium in a Civilian Reactor Is Dangerous and Unnecessary." *Scientific American*, October 20, 2023, https://www.scientificamerican.com/article/u-s-plan-to-put-weapons-grade-uranium-in-a-civilian-reactor-is-dangerous-and-unnecessary/.

Weber, Ella. "How Did Nuclear Weapons Get on My Reservation?" *Scientific American*, November 14, 2023, https://www.scientificamerican.com/podcast/episode/how-did-nuclear-weapons-get-on-my-reservation1/.

CITATIONS

1.1 What Was the Manhattan Project? by Tom Metcalfe (July 21, 2023); 1.2 Manhattan Project Plutonium, Lost to Obscurity, Recovered by Scientists by Andy Extance (January 15, 2015); 1.3 Nuclear-Testing 'Downwinders' Speak about History and Fear by Sarah Scoles (January 27, 2022); 1.4 The U.S. Must Take Responsibility for Nuclear Fallout in the Marshall Islands by Hart Rapaport & Ivana Nikolić Hughes (April 4, 2022); 1.5 The Future of Nuclear Power: Let a Thousand Flowers Bloom by Ashutosh Jogalekar (December 6, 2013); 2.1 First U.S. Small Nuclear Reactor Design Is Approved by Dave Levitan (September 9, 2020); 2.2 So-Called Next-Generation Nuclear Power Plants Are Being Oversold by Elliott Negin (July 23, 2021); 2.3 What Is the Future of Fusion Energy? by Philip Ball (June 1, 2023); 2.4 World's Largest Fusion Project Is in Big Trouble, New Documents Reveal by Charles Seife (June 15, 2023); 3.1 How Nuclear Power Can Stop Global Warming by David Biello (December 12, 2013); 3.2 We Should Be More Worried about Climate Change Than We Are about Nuclear Power by Wade Roush (July 1, 2019); 3.3 New Nuclear Power Plants Are Unlikely to Stop the Climate Crisis by Naomi Oreskes (February 1, 2022); 4.1 What Happens During a Nuclear Meltdown? by John Matson (March 15, 2011); 4.2 Deconstructing John Miller's Arguments Against Nuclear Energy in the *New York Times* by Ashutosh Jogalekar (August 23, 2013); 4.3 Chernobyl Didn't Kill Nuclear Power by Frank N. von Hippel (April 1, 2016); 4.4 The Risks of Russian Attacks near Ukraine's Nuclear Power Plants by Andrea Thompson (March 5, 2022); 5.1 A (Radioactive) Cut in the Earth That Will Not Stay Closed by Tom Zoellner (March 27, 2009); 5.2 Spent Nuclear Fuel: A Trash Heap Deadly for 250,000 Years or a Renewable Energy Source? by David Biello (January 28, 2009); 5.3 Abandoned Uranium Mines: An "Overwhelming Problem" in the Navajo Nation by Francie Diep (December 30, 2010); 5.4 Hanford Nuclear Waste Cleanup Plant May Be Too Dangerous by Valerie Brown (May 9, 2013); 5.5 Nuclear Waste Is Piling Up. Does the U.S. Have a Plan? by Allison Macfarlane & Rodney C. Ewing (March 6, 2023); 6.1 Behind the Scenes at a U.S. Factory Building New Nuclear Bombs by Sarah Scoles (December 1, 2023); 6.2 Who Would Take the Brunt of an Attack on U.S. Nuclear Missile Silos? by Sébastien Philippe (December 1, 2023); 7.1 The Workings of an Ancient Nuclear Reactor by Alex P. Meshik (January 26, 2009); 7.2 NASA's 'Nuclear Option' May Be Crucial for Getting Humans to Mars by David W. Brown (January 27, 2022).

Each author biography was accurate at the time the article was originally published.

INDEX